Lies, Damned Lies, and Cost Accounting

Lies, Damned Lies, and Cost Accounting

How Capacity Management Enables Improved Cost and Cash Flow Management

Dr. Reginald Tomas Lee, Sr.

BEP BUSINESS EXPERT PRESS

Lies, Damned Lies, and Cost Accounting: How Capacity Management Enables Improved Cost and Cash Flow Management

Copyright © Business Expert Press, LLC, 2016

First published in 2016 by
Business Expert Press, LLC
222 East 46th Street, New York, NY 10017
www.businessexpertpress.com

ISBN-13: 978-1-63157-065-0 (paperback)
ISBN-13: 978-1-63157-066-7 (e-book)

Business Expert Press Managerial Accounting Collection

Collection ISSN: 2152-2795 (print)
Collection ISSN: 2151-2817 (electronic)

Cover and interior design by S4Carlisle Publishing Services
Private Ltd., Chennai, India

First edition: 2016

10 9 8 7 6 5 4 3 2 1

Dedication

To my wife and better half, Tamara

Abstract

Business leaders rely on accounting data such as profit and calculated costs as a guide to whether they are making money. Should they?

Accounting was designed to report financial performance not model cash flow. Accruals can disconnect cash flow from the timing and extent to which it occurs. Statements of cash flow do not provide insight into what was bought and how efficiently it was used. Accounting costs and profits are not absolute; they change based on the model you use to calculate them.

To manage cash, you must manage what you buy and how effectively you use it. The largest expenditure for most companies is capacity; space, labor, materials, equipment, and technology. Unless you model and manage capacity effectively, you will not achieve the cash flow results you seek.

This book introduces capacity management, describes cash flow dynamics, and offers ideas about how to manage each both. After reading it, you will be able to see, understand, and manage cash flow as never before.

Keywords

Accounting, Activity based costing, Activity cost, Average costing, Break-even, Capacity, Capacity accounting, Capacity cost, Capacity management, Cash, Cash flow, Cash management, Constraint, Cost, Cost accounting, Cost allocation, Cost assignment, Cost curve, Costing, Cost improvement, Cost management, Cost reduction, Costs, Customer profitability, Demand, Demand management, Dynamic capacity, Economic costs, Efficiency, Effectiveness, Explicit cost dynamics, Goldratt, Input capacity, Isocost, Isocost curve, Just-in-time, Lean, Lean accounting, Management accounting, Managerial accounting, Metrics, Operational improvement, Optimization, Output capacity, Performance, Performance improvement, Performance management , Process costing, Process design, Process Improvement, Process optimization, Product costing, Product profitability, Productivity, Profit, Return on investment, ROI, Service costing, Service profitability, Six sigma, Standard costing, Static Capacity, Theory of Constraints, Throughput accounting, Total quality management, Unit profit, WACA, Worth, Worth and capacity analysis

Contents

Acknowledgments

I must first thank my family for allowing me the time, space, and motivation to do this project. My wife, Tamara, was not thrilled by the prospect of my writing another book, but reluctantly agreed and provided incredible support throughout the entire process. I can't thank her enough for standing by me and being an incredible wife, mother, friend, motivator, and drill sergeant. Thank you, Tamara. You're an amazing woman.

The kids, Sunny (master editor), A-Mac, Bella, Wokka, Toughman, and Dukeus (I almost never call the kids by their real names unless I'm mad) were all troopers in making sure I had the space, inspiration, and love necessary to complete the book. Rudolph (father) and Fred (mother) were early inspirations. My father was an accountant and an incredible role model, while my mother was an extraordinary educator, motivator, and friend. We miss them both dearly. My sister, Wynnette, and my brother, Marc, continue to inspire and support. I'd certainly not be who I am without them.

I thank my academic peers and reviewers: Dr. Joe Castellano, Dr. Bertie Greer, and Dr. Ken Merchant for their reviews and support; Dr. Glen Johnson for his ongoing conversations and support and Dr. Thomas Scott for his detailed thoughts and feedback as well. Their ideas and input have greatly influenced this book.

There are a few people I thank professionally. First is Michael Fournier of the Society of Cost Management for his insistence on my writing this book. If it weren't for Michael, there would be no book. Scott Isenberg of Business Expert Press has been fantastic to work with. Finally, I've worked with some great folks when publishing work related to this book. Thanks to Ed Stone, Barry Brinker, Paul Sharman, Michael Hughes, Jim Edwards, Beth Gongde, and Ashlie Carlson.

There are other friends I thank as well. First, I'd like to thank my friend and former student Marianne Novac Davis. We've done some projects together and I hope to do more. I deeply value her ideas and friendship on many levels. Angela, Jordan, Scot, Xan, Deanna, and

Libby were all very supportive throughout this process, especially on those long Saturday afternoons. Rob and Tony from Four80East provided the tunes that helped inspire as always. Great guys, great band, great music! Thanks guys.

Finally, as always, I thank my friend Pepe for his years of influence and support during my writing projects.

Introduction

I wrote this book for the curious business man and woman. You are the ones who are always looking to learn more. Through your learning, you've likely realized that there is too much focus on accounting data and not enough on understanding the factors that influence the data. You see your colleagues, bosses, peers in other companies, and those who work for you make decisions that make you scratch your head even though the analyses may support that decision from an accounting perspective.

Although this is not an accounting book, I suspect, based on early feedback and from those who have read my other works, that many accountants will not only read this book and gain insights into the numbers they deal with, but also the limitations of accounting data and how it may keep your organization from moving forward. This book will create a language and an approach that will allow you to align with operations to create a team to move your organization forward.

This is not really an operations book either. Although many operations-based ideas such as capacity management, efficiency, and productivity are addressed, the purpose is to show how these factors influence how your company spends money and manages what it bought. You'll see that you can model everything you do operationally with the tools in this book, and you'll be able to understand and model the cash flow dynamics of what you do and the improvements you want to make.

There will be people who dislike this book, and that is ok. The foundations of this book are based purely in mathematics. Over the past two decades of developing these ideas and sharing them with a global audience, people have fought the ideas and have said mean things to and about me, but no one has refuted the math. That is what matters to me; developing a robust tool that will help others.

The book is written under the premise that cash flow is what is most important for a business. It is broken down into three parts. The first part explains why the income statement and certain accounting practices are not good proxies for managing cash flow. Many accountants already know some of this, although many do not know why. The second part introduces the idea and importance of capacity. For most companies, this is where you spend most of your cash, yet is is widely misunderstood and ignored in accounting and, in fact, business at large. In my opinion, this is the most overlooked component of how businesses operate, function, and influence cash flow decisions. The third part deals with applying some of the ideas from my first book, *Explicit Cost Dynamics,* to offer leaders ways to model capacity and cash flow, and to make better decisions with the information.

I thank you for giving me the opportunity to share these ideas with you. I hope you will find them valuable and useful in your work.

PART 1

CHAPTER 1

Blue Pill or Red Pill?

What would happen if the world you believed to be true was not? Every interaction with every person, every emotion, every thought, feelings of joy, and pain did not exist? How would you react? How would you feel? The sky not only isn't blue; it may not exist at all. If the truth painted a very different picture of reality than you expected, would you be willing to accept it, or would you ignore it and return to the world of false reality?

The movie, The Matrix, creates such a scenario. People live in a world like ours, or the one we believe we live in. They see blue skies, they smell the scent of freshly cut grass, and they experience love. However, in reality, none of this exists. None of it is real.

> *What is real? How do you define "real"? If you're talking about what you can feel, what you can smell, what you can taste and see, then "real" is simply electrical signals interpreted by your brain.[1]*

Machines, the antagonists in the movie, have created a computer program called The Matrix, and its purpose is to mimic the reality humans believe they are living in. Humans believe they are living their lives, waking up, going to work, having social and spiritual lives. The machines have created a situation where the humans believe this is their reality, that they are free. But they aren't. In reality, the machines have physical and mental control of the humans. The humans are captured and living in a suspended state that is generally beyond their knowledge and control. They are being harvested as a source of energy for machines that control the world. The Matrix creates this false reality by manipulating electrical signals sent to the

---

[1]The Matrix. Dir. Andy Wachowski and Larry Wachowski. Warner Bros. Pictures, 1999. DVD.

brain, thereby altering the perception of what is real. The mind, as they say, cannot tell the difference between what is real and what is imaginary. The Matrix controlled the "reality" the humans perceived. Instead of a bright world of friends and laughter, each individual was isolated and alone in a dark world, existing only in a pod by themselves.

There are a number of humans who are not captured and controlled by The Matrix who know about the situation. One is a fighter named Morpheus. He has a quest to find someone who could destroy The Matrix and free humans from being slaves to the machines. There is a point in the movie where Morpheus finds and develops a relationship with one potential freedom fighter named Neo. Neo is captured, but somehow concludes something is wrong with the world. However, he is not quite sure what it is and how pervasive it is. Morpheus believes Neo can defeat The Matrix. There is a scene early in the movie where Morpheus offers to explain The Matrix to Neo, hoping to have him join their cause, but he knows Neo might not be ready to find out the truth about what is happening to humans including himself. To prepare Neo, Morpheus extends his arms and opens his hands revealing a red pill and a blue pill. He offers Neo a choice of taking either pill saying,

> *This is your last chance. After this, there is no turning back. You take the blue pill—the story ends, you wake up in your bed and believe whatever you want to believe. You take the red pill—you stay in Wonderland and I show you how deep the rabbit-hole goes.*[2]

So What?

When it comes to business and understanding financial numbers, we are faced with a similar question: What is real? Is something real because we are told it is real? Because it is calculated mathematically using a standard approach or formula? Does creating a better way to perform a task that is, itself, questionable, make the result real?

In business, there are two worlds, just as there were in The Matrix. Each world attempts to describe the financial performance of an organization.

---

[2]Ibid.

There is one world, like the accounting version of The Matrix where accounting numbers dictate, influence, and arguably control management thinking and action. That is a world where costing things such as products, services, activities, and work output is a critical part of the thinking and actions. Never mind the notion that the idea itself may be flawed. In this world, it is a panacea.

Then there is the world of reality—real math, real modeling, leading to a clearer understanding of business structure and operations, and this enables more effective management decision-making. In this context, this world, accounting is a reporting tool, and nothing more. Leaders look to understand the facts of what is going on in their organizations and choose to live and operate outside the accounting Matrix preferring to focus on real operational data and the financial data that result directly from it. They go into the accounting Matrix only when required to deal with the false reality that has been created.

You, like Neo, have a choice. Your blue pill is to put this book down and continue living without the knowledge of how damaging the improper use and interpretation of accounting data can be, and how to improve the effectiveness of your management skills and decision-making. Reading this book is your red pill. By choosing to read this book, you will begin to understand how the improper use and representation of your company's cash data leads you to realize that your business reality is not, in fact, real at all. You will see that accounting tools, especially in the form of cost accounting, are damaging to your ability to comprehend what is really going on in your business. Like The Matrix without the evil intent, cost accounting is pervasive and affects the thinking and decision-making of people throughout society, both in the business world and outside the business world without their knowledge. Cost accounting alters the perception of reality. The result? The world has seen lives, families, companies, communities, and economies destroyed by poor decisions made by otherwise intelligent leaders with accounting data as a basis.

The purpose of this book is to expose some of these practices, help you understand the implications behind them, and offer you a way out.

Once you understand these ideas, you will not be able to turn back. You will be able to operate within accounting just like Morpheus, Neo, and other freedom fighters operated within The Matrix. They went in and out gathering information they needed to support their cause. You will know that this world, built by accounting data, has significant limitations and does not reflect the true reality. This is your warning. You can take the blue pill and live a professional life unknowing by putting this book down, or you can take the red pill and see the world of business differently.

CHAPTER 2

The Foundation

Let's begin with a foundation on which we can agree. There are two financial things every company must do both to survive and be in compliance with the law. It doesn't matter the size of the company, its industry, or whether it is for profit or not for profit. The company must generate cash and it must report its earnings to the government for a number of reasons including, but not limited to taxes, providing financial performance data if the company is public, and as proof of financial transactions for nonprofits. Failure to do either or both of these will limit your company's ability to exist long term. I trust you will agree with me on these two ideas. Let's look at each of these individually.

Generating Cash

Generating cash, cash flow, is the lifeblood of any company. All companies need positively flowing cash to ensure they are able to survive and, ideally to grow.

Generating cash comes from two primary sources. One source is investors who infuse cash in various ways including debt and money for equity. The other is to make more money than you are spending by selling products and services. The former may involve getting capital to address a tactical or strategic need. A key consideration is that this money is expected to be paid back in some way. Although it may provide needed sources for survival or growth, it comes at a price. The latter is a requirement and necessary capability for all companies.

Reporting Earnings

The government requires companies to report their earnings. In the United States, some may have to report to governing agencies such as the

Securities and Exchange Commission (SEC) and, at a minimum, to the Internal Revenue Service (IRS). To ensure everyone does so in a standard, consistent way, there are rules and guidelines established by these agencies. The primary objective of the reports is to represent what the company did, according to the agency guidelines, over a fixed analysis period. Doing this will help the company describe how well it performed during the analysis period. This information may also be used by the investment community as a way to understand and assess company performance. Whether looking at reports prepared for the SEC or looking at statements for loans, this information becomes a basis for how lenders assess the financial viability of your company. The most commonly used are the income statement, the balance sheet, and the statement of cash flows. Often, we focus on the income statement—the description of profits and losses.

Abstractly, the way your business operates is seen in Exhibit 2.1. In this diagram, you see that the company buys resources and performs work, and the desire is that this process leaves the company in the position to make more money than it spent. When this happens, you had a generally positive analysis period. There may be unmet expectations about *how much* money was made, but in general, the objective is to be profitable—to make more money.

We consider the income statement to determine whether we made money. The basic idea is that if the revenues you generate are greater than costs you have, you have made money. Logically, this makes sense. If you make $100 and you spend $60, you have $40 left. This information allows you to make decisions such as how much you have to spend on other things. The problem is the income statement does not tell you how much money you made. In fact, the whole notion of profit may have little to do with making money at all.

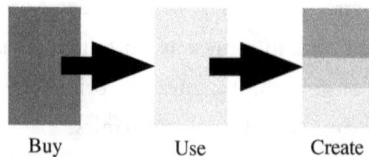

Buy   Use   Create

Exhibit 2.1 When we buy a resource, we have a defined amount we will have access to. It is from what we buy that we do work to create output in various forms. Sometimes the output is products or services, it may be information, and it could be offices created from space we lease

CHAPTER 3

Profit has Little to do with Making Money

Everyone talks about profit, and we assume that profit and making money are synonymous. The question is: Are they? Making money represents the amount of money you generate. It is cash and timing based. How much money you make is determined by the net cash you bring in over a given time period. Determining how much cash you generated should be tied directly to when you spend and receive cash. You cannot talk about how much money you made this year by considering what you're going to spend next year and what you received last year. This notion is critically important. If you want to know how much money you have or expect to have you must consider the cash that comes in and leaves during the time period considered. *It doesn't make sense to think about managing cash flow when the timing of cash transactions is eliminated from consideration.* Remember this line.

We generally calculate profit using the profit equation. This general equation is well-known to all in business and in many other aspects of life. That equation is

$$\text{Profit} = \text{Revenues} - \text{Costs} \qquad (3.1)$$

The assumption, again, is that profit is synonymous with making money. For profit to represent making money, though, the timing and cash flows have to be in alignment. They aren't. There are six reasons why:

1. Revenue recognition
2. The practice of costing
3. The definition of costs

4. Believing efficiency and waste reduction lowers costs
5. Misunderstanding inventory value
6. Depreciation

Each of these will be mentioned briefly here. However, because of the depth of the issue involved, each topic has earned its own chapter.

Revenue Recognition

The first idea that challenges whether profit can represent making money is revenue recognition. The rules of financial accounting allow flexibility for when you can recognize money from sales transactions.[1] Assume, for instance, that we are looking at the current calendar year to report your financials. You may sell something today, but not receive payment for it until next year. If you recognize the revenue this year and use this information to calculate profit for this year, but you haven't received the money, there is a disconnect between revenue reported and cash you've made.

The Practice of Costing

Costing supposes products, services, and work activities have financial values associated with their creation or execution. The assumption is that this financial value has ties to money spent, therefore affecting cash. If costs go up or down, that change will directly affect cash and profit. Interestingly, different approaches can look at the same expenses and use of resources, and calculate *different* costs. The idea you can calculate different costs from the same data and information should suggest that costs do not represent cash. If they did, there would be one cost because you spent your money and transacted business one way.

---

[1]Generally Accepted Accounting Principles, or GAAP, allows income statements to be prepared on an accrual bases. The accrual process provides guidelines regarding the timing of recognizing revenues and the reporting of expenses, irrespective of when the cash transaction takes place.

Cost Definitions

I used to ask myself, "What is a cost?" Costs can be money spent on an item you buy. In this case, there is a financial transaction. A cost can also be a financial representation of the consumption of capacity. For instance, when you calculate the cost of a meeting or to process an invoice, you are assigning a dollar value to the use of something you've already bought or agreed to buy, such as an employee's time. There is no financial transaction involved with the meeting or the invoice; hence, no exchange of cash, but many consider this cost to be the equivalent of a cash transaction. The notion that there is no cash transaction associated with certain types of costs suggests there can be a disconnect between costs and cash.[2]

Efficiency

We are taught, and therefore assume, that increasing efficiency reduces costs. This is often the basis for many types of activities related to process and product cost reductions. It is assumed that by increasing our efficiency, our costs will go down. Common examples are lean, Six Sigma, and waste reduction activities, where the objective is to lower costs by becoming more efficient. The question is: Does efficiency affect cash? The answer is: Not directly. It can enable changes in cash. More on this later. For now, consider your own salary. If someone makes you 10 percent more efficient, will you be paid less? The answer is: No. But you now have more time to do other things. If you use space more efficiently, will your lease costs decrease? No, but you have more space to use for other things. When companies talk about increasing efficiency with lean and Six Sigma projects, they will quote huge savings in costs. These costs, more often than not, will not be realized in cash, directly, and in many cases will not even make it to the financial

---

[2]Complicating this further is the notion of unexpired and expired costs. Let's say you buy something. Whatever part of it you realize benefit from, it is now an expired cost. If you have not realized benefit from it, the cost is considered unexpired. So the cost is determined not when you spent the money but when you received value from it.

statements as a cost savings.[3] This creates a disconnect between proposed cost savings from efficiency improvements and how these savings translate into cash flow savings.

Inventory

Companies spend money when building inventory. For example, they have labor they are paying for, materials that they bought to use, and they have the space they paid for to build the inventory. However, it is a very real possibility that the money spent building the inventory today will not be included in the cost calculations for profit today and will not be included until a subsequent accounting period.[4] In other words, it is possible you can spend money today and it will not go into your profit calculations until years later. This creates a potential disconnect between when you spend cash and when it is used to calculate profit.

Depreciation

When you buy something that is depreciated, the rate of depreciation has nothing to do with the amount and timing of your cash payments. This creates yet another disconnect between profit and making money.

In the end, profit, from a reporting perspective, is a calculated value, created with many assumptions that abide by guidelines created by governing bodies. Those rules and guidelines create a scenario where accounting cannot represent cash flow.[5] Remember the statement regarding timing that I asked you to remember in Chapter 2? Here is where that statement comes into play. Making money has only to do with whether you are bringing in more money than you are making in a given period. If your objective is generating cash, profit is the wrong proxy to use to help you understand whether you are making money or not. Let's understand these more.

---

[3]Reginald Tomas Lee, "How we Overstate ROI on Improvement Projects," *Cost Management*, November/December, 2015.
[4]Another example of accruals.
[5]This is especially true when using accrual accounting.

CHAPTER 4

Revenue Recognition

The first value in the profit equation is revenue or sales. This number represents the financial value for the products and services you've sold. It is from this number that costs are subtracted to calculate profit. The challenge with revenue recognition is that there does not have to be alignment between when you sell something, when you recognize the revenue (I will be paid), and when you receive cash (I have been paid) (Exhibit 4.1). The most common such situation is one where you sell an item and recognize revenue without receiving payment. This is regularly the case for companies that sell items with payment terms—"pay us in 30 or 60 days." In these cases, if you sell something in December and recognize the sales transaction in that year, it is possible that you will not collect the cash until the subsequent year in a completely different accounting period.

The worse your receivables situation is, the worse this problem can become. Companies with large days sales outstanding, say 90 days as an example, have, on average, a 90-day gap between when they sell their product or service and when they receive payment for it. In the absolute worst-case scenario, the payment is not received at all. You sell your product or service, acknowledge the revenue, and receive nothing for it.

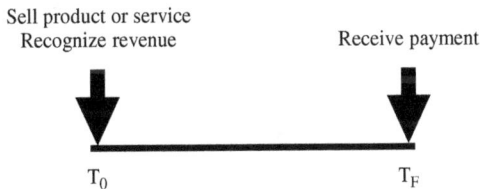

Sell product or service
Recognize revenue   Receive payment

T_0 T_F

Exhibit 4.1 The challenge with revenue recognition and cash flow is that you can recognize revenue for profit calculation purposes and receive payment at a different time. This creates a disconnect between the revenue used to calculate profit and the cash you receive to run the company

Of course, there are accounting concessions available for such situations; however, clearly, this situation does not reflect the cash flow dynamics of what truly happened and neither do the concessions.

If revenue were truly tied to cash, it would be recognized when, and in what amount, you receive the cash. There are times when the rules and regulations even discourage this behavior such as with gift cards. With gift cards, companies are not allowed to recognize the cash received when the cards are purchased by consumers. Although there are reasons for establishing these regulations, and they make sense for what they're trying to accomplish, this, and understanding the reason and logic behind the rules, doesn't change the fact that the transaction does not align with cash flow.

If you use sales as a proxy for incoming cash, it is important to understand this. How and when you receive cash may have little to do with the accounting number you report when you sold that item. If you don't consider the timing and the terms, your revenue numbers will be disconnected from your cash flow.

CHAPTER 5

The Practice of Costing

The question here is: Are costs aligned with cash flowing away from your company, and if not, why not? Costs should, by their very nature, be aligned to cash leaving, but they are not in all cases. Costing and cost accounting are based on false ideas, false relationships, and on the inappropriate use of math. These issues will be discussed in detail throughout the rest of the book. The purpose of this chapter is only to demonstrate that costs, themselves, do not align with cash.

Pick an arbitrary time period. It begins on the first day of the analysis period—a month, a year—and ends on the last day of that period. During that time, you spend money buying things, consuming things, and doing work. Let's think about the scenario. At the end of the analysis, what you spent, how much you spent, what you bought, and how you used it have been determined. Every action and transaction is now set in stone. There is only one description; one representation of what happened. When you look back, you didn't hire one or two people. You hired two. You didn't have 200 or 300 meetings. You had 273 meetings. You didn't create 75 or 80 products to sell. You created 76. Everything that happened during that period can be documented in retrospect. Then comes costing.

If we agree on the idea that there is one and only one description of the past, let's think about the costing aspect. There are many different approaches to costing products, services, processes, and activities. Each one emphasizes something different. Standard costing may emphasize different aspects of cost assignments and relationships than activity-based costing. Lean accounting is different from throughput accounting. Yet, the fact remains that each approach is attempting to assign the cost of what was purchased either before or during the analysis period, to what you did and created, all in the name of determining *the* cost of a product, service, process, or activity.

The result is a puzzling scenario. When trying to cost a product, service, or activity in an analysis period, since each approach available to use assigns costs differently, you can create different values for the cost. The cost of a pen you manufacture, for example, may be calculated to be $1.12 with standard costing, $1.27 with activity-based costing, and $1.35 with overhead costs spread equally. This can be disturbing but understandable because each approach emphasizes different things. However, even if you talk to three people about using one approach such as activity-based costing, you will likely receive three different costs as well.[1] What is even more puzzling is that if you use a fairly standard procedure, the approach will pass an audit performed by your CPA (certified public accounting) firm. Had you used another standard approach and calculated a different number, it, too, would pass the audit. So, what is the right answer?

Let's recap. During an analysis period, one set of spending transactions and one set of activities occurred, and the result was the creation of a unique description of work and output. Yet different costs for the exact same thing can be created. The difference can be due to the approach used, but even using the same approach, one can calculate different values. One must ask: If the desire to describe one thing results in multiple answers, how effective is any one of the answers at explaining what happened? If you walk into a physician's office not knowing how tall you are and they tell you that you're 5ft 9inches, you can feel good about that number. But if they tell you that you're 5ft 9inches, 6ft 4inches, or 5ft 3inches depending on the technique they used, you will question the results. And if using the same approach, say a yardstick, and the answer is that you're either 5ft 9inches or 6ft 1inch, again, you'll question results. Segal's law suggests a man with a watch knows what time it is. A man with two watches has no idea.[2]

If cash were spent one way, one set of activities occurred, and you are trying to determine the cost of these activities, logically, there would be one and only one cost. If there can be many costs coming from one set of data describing what happened, how can they all be aligned to cash flow?

---

[1] Often, the differences are tied to the scope of activities being considered and choices about how to interpret and assign costs.

[2] "When Can Segal's Law Be Applied?" - *Quora*. Web. 22 Nov. 2015.

CHAPTER 6

Cost Definitions

Cost is an interesting term. It is something that is extremely common to discuss in many settings, business or not. We talk about the cost to make a product, the cost to have a meeting, the cost to process an invoice, or to acquire a new customer. My wife and I even discuss and debate costs related to cooking meals! I would offer, however, that the business world does not understand costs to the extent it believes it does. Also, I would offer we cannot regularly and easily discern the two types of costs and why some costs have absolutely nothing to do with cash. Let me demonstrate.

Let's say I have a pen I'd like to sell to you. We agree on a price of $50. I sell the pen to you, you give me $50. There is a transaction with a clear exchange of cash. Now, as the person selling that pen, I, thinking like a cost traditionalist, would like to know how profitable the transaction was—how much money did I make? To determine this, I would have to calculate a cost and plug it into the profit equation.

The first problem is calculating the cost. As mentioned in the last chapter, there really is no single cost. One approach may result in a cost of $25, another $19.72, and have a third of $27.63. Let's say for the sake of discussion, we use $25. Logically, if costs were tied to cash flow, there should be a $25 transaction representing the money involved in making that pen, and I should make $25 in cash after the transaction is completed. That doesn't happen. Why?

To calculate the cost of my pen, I had to make assumptions and create relationships that don't exist. I'll give you an example. Remember way back in time when we used to have telephones hardwired into our homes? To get access to local phone calls, we would pay a local access fee. Assume the access fee for service is $25, and with this $25, we could make unlimited number of local phone calls. However, if we wanted to call someone outside of local area, we had to pay a long-distance fee. Let's say the long-distance fee was $0.10 per minute. A 10-minute call would cost $1. Quick. How much would a 10-minute local call cost?

I bet you didn't come up with that answer quite so quickly if you came up with one at all. Why? Because with long-distance calls, you were buying time, minutes, so there was a direct relationship between how many minutes you bought and what you paid. There is no such relationship between buying access and what you do with the access. This includes both making calls and attributes about the call such as its length in time or distance from you. The cost to you is $25, whether you make no calls or an infinite number of them as long as you are within the service area. To get the cost of a 10-minute local phone call, since no relationship exists, you have to create one—make it up. Since you're making up this relationship, it is arbitrary. The only thing we know for sure from a cash transaction perspective is that the $25 has to be paid so that you can make a local calls. Once you go beyond this, you are headed into the realm of making up a false reality to calculate the cost of a call.

How much faith can you put into a number that was made up by creating an arbitrary relationship between two logically and mathematically independent things? How much value does it and can it have? You'd think none. Yet this is what we do every day.

Back to the pen. To calculate the cost of my pen, I will have to create a relationship that is similar to one that may be used when calculating the cost of a local call. What I pay someone who is making the pen has nothing to do with the pens they make if they are paid by the hour. It is based on how much access to them I buy. The cash transaction is tied to paying them for their time. Eight hours is more expensive to buy than seven. The same with materials. I buy materials and have them to create output—pens. As with labor, the price you pay for material has nothing to do with how it's used, only its price and how much you buy. But to determine the cost of the pens, we must create an artificial relationship between what you bought, access, and how you used it, create output. This results in a mathematically false financial relationship between what you paid to have people, materials, and space to do work, and the cost value assigned to the work created by using them. The relationship created represents the consumption of labor, materials, space, and other factors, puts a dollar value on this consumption, and calls it a cost. The $25 represents one interpretation of the value of the inputs that are used to create the pen. When I make one more pen, am I giving someone $25? If so, to whom am I giving the money? If I don't make the pen, does it mean I saved $25? No. These costs don't just go away. I still have the people, the material vendor, and the lease to pay.

So what should you conclude from this? The reality is that there are two types of costs. One is the cost that involves an exchange of cash. After this exchange, you're either richer or poorer, depending on whether you were giving or receiving the money. In other published materials, I have referred to this as *cost as expense,* and it is a cash flow cost.[1] I will use the designation $cost_C$ to reflect cash flow costs. The second cost is *cost as effort,* and this cost represents putting a monetary value on the consumption of space, labor, equipment, materials, and technology—things you buy in anticipation of demand or use. In this case, there's no financial transaction, so there is no cash involved. Costs that have no cash value will be referred to as $cost_{NC}$, with the NC referencing the idea that it is not cash.

It is critically important that you understand the differences between $cost_C$ and $cost_{NC}$. Because they're both called costs, there is an assumption that they belong together logically, mathematically, and, therefore, financially. They do not. They're very different values and they represent very different things, so combining them into one number and calling them all *costs* is a dangerous practice. Let me explain.

Practically all companies embark on efforts to manage or reduce costs. They buy expensive IT systems, invest in developing Six Sigma black belts, and focus on lean initiatives to improve financial performance; all to reduce costs. Executives claim savings opportunities that seem to be excessively large, such as $50–75 million just from transforming a finance group. This amount is used to cover the $25 million it costs to implement the software using your favorite big consulting firm. How often do these projects pan out as planned? How often do these huge business cases lead to the numbers they promise? These sometimes huge numbers should result in numbers you can see on your financial

---

[1] See, for example, Reginald Tomas Lee, "Making Better Offshoring and Onshoring Decisions," *Journal of Corporate Accounting & Finance,* September/October 2014.

statements, right? That $3 million you saved because you can process invoices faster and have a cleaner general ledger *should show up someplace*. They do not nearly as often as the projects are approved. Why? Two reasons. First, the costs and cost savings were calculated and interpreted improperly. Second, these values, as a result, were not truly financial values. Let's discuss both.

Calculated Costs

When calculating savings, if your costs were calculated using an arbitrary relationship between what you bought and what you created, the cost is related to the consumption of capacity and is, therefore, $cost_{NC}$. When you change how much capacity you're using, it changes the value of $cost_{NC}$. If you use less capacity, the value of the capacity consumed does go down; hence you lower $cost_{NC}$. Recall, however, that the cost you pay to have access to capacity, $cost_C$, and what you do with it are independent. If you interpret this non-cash cost, $cost_{NC}$, as a cash cost, you will create a false and inflated savings opportunity.[2]

The Numbers Aren't Financial

These calculated savings $cost_{NC}$, will often not be seen on the income statement. When looking to improve a process such as accounts payable using automation technology, you may improve $cost_{NC}$. However, the labor that may be improved is reported in aggregate as salary. Since the improvement will not affect salary, it will not show up on the income statement. It is possible that cost of goods sold improvements may show up on the income statement, but you will need to look at the entire picture. You can lower the average $cost_{NC}$ for a pen by making a lot of them, but if your production exceeds demand, your margin on each pen sold may be better; but you may have spent an excessive amount of cash building what may be unneeded products. Consider this. How can it be cheaper to make 20 pens than it is to make five? More of everything

---

[2]Reginald Tomas Lee, "How we Overstate ROI on Improvement Projects" *Cost Management*, November/December 2015.

is required. Of course, the cost$_{NC}$ per unit is lower, but what does this mean? If there were demand for five, would you still choose to build 20? If not, why not, if it's cheaper financially? If it is a financial value and it is better for you, why wouldn't you choose to overproduce? Remember this thought.

By not understanding cost$_C$ versus cost$_{NC}$, and by not acknowledging cost$_{NC}$ has nothing to do with cash, you're guaranteed to promise results you will not achieve. If you promise a total of $5 million in savings from your IT project, $1 million is cost$_C$ and $4 million cost$_{NC}$, the cash potential is $1 million. If you assume they're the same and you expect $5 million in cash, you will be disappointed. The cost that affects cash flow is cost$_C$. That is it. Cost$_{NC}$ as a cash value is a mirage, and should not be considered equally with cost$_C$ in cash flow discussions. They are as different as rocks and trees.

CHAPTER 7

Understanding Efficiency

Efficiency is an interesting concept. It is one of those ideas that people believe they understand, but when talking to them about efficiency, there doesn't seem to be a clear and agreed upon understanding of what it really is. There are common beliefs about efficiency, however. One common belief is that by increasing efficiency you will lower costs. Many programs focus on improving efficiency in the name of reducing costs. This is actually a driving factor behind the famed Toyota Production System, the precursor to well known concepts such as lean.[1] The question is: Does it really work? The answer is: Yes and no.

To begin, let's define efficiency in a way that will be used throughout the book. Efficiency is simply output divided by input as seen in Equation 7.1:

$$\text{Efficiency} = \text{Output} / \text{Input} \qquad (7.1)$$

Consider fuel efficiency with your vehicle, miles per gallon. The gallon you start with is the input, and the distance you can travel on the gallon becomes your output. The car that can go 30 miles on a single gallon of gas is considered more efficient than the car that can go only 10. When you try to increase fuel efficiency, the objective is either to see if you can go farther, increase your output, on a gallon of gas or to see if you can go the same distance with less gas —outputs and inputs.

The same notion applies to work and your company. If you have two people who do the same thing for an hour, the one who creates the most

---

[1]Taiichi Ohno, the primary architect of the Toyota Product System, suggested that the goal of the TPS is cost reduction. This is highlighted in Taiichi Ohno, *Toyota Production System: Beyond Large Scale Production* (Cambridge MA: Productivity Press, 1988), 62.

output in that hour is more efficient. For example, if you have two people handling customer service calls, the one who answers the most calls in an hour is mathematically and technically more efficient. It doesn't mean they are better at doing their job, as one possible reason one is more efficient could be they avoid difficult situations that take more time to resolve. This may lead to a negative experience for the customer. However, according to the math definition, they are still more efficient.

To increase efficiency, you improve the ratio of output to input. As with the gas example, a few paragraphs earlier, if you have someone handling 10 customer service calls per hour, increasing the output to 11 per hour increases their efficiency. Doing 10 calls in less than an hour will also improve your efficiency. The question is: Where does the cost-reduction come from?

Let's assume you wanted to calculate the cost per call in this scenario. If the reps are paid by the hour and not by the call, you are back to the situation in Chapter 6, where you have to create a financial relationship between what you pay them and what they do. If the rep makes $20 per hour, let's assume an average cost per call can be calculated by dividing the $20 for the hour by the number of calls made during the hour. This is, of course, $cost_{NC}$. At 10 calls, the cost per call is calculated to be $2. At 11 calls, cost per call is calculated to be $1.82, $0.18 cheaper per call.

The $cost_{NC}$ goes down, but what does this imply? You still pay the agent $20, whether they make 10 calls, 11 calls, no calls, or 1,000 calls. The cash you spend to get the 11 calls versus the 10 is exactly the same. There are no cash implications associated with the number of calls you make. This further demonstrates the independence of the cost of buying capacity, $cost_C$, and what it does.

This should tell you three things. First, the cost per call is not a cash-based value as discussed in Chapter 6. It is $cost_{NC}$. What you spent to get 11 calls is the same as what you spend to get 10. Second, efficiency is the math inverse of average cost per call (Equation 7.2).[2] If the hour is input, then the $20 you paid, too, is input. Eleven calls are more efficient than 10 because you got more calls, output, for the same input, $20. Now,

---

[2]There is a deeper dive into this relationship in Appendix A.

consider cost per call. Mathematically, the average cost per call is input divided by output, which is the opposite of efficiency (Equation 7.3)

$$\text{Efficiency} = \text{Output} / \text{Input} \qquad (7.1)$$

$$\text{Efficiency} = \text{Calls} / \text{Cost (e.g., 11 calls/\$20)}$$
$$\text{Average cost per call} = \text{Cost} / \text{Calls (e.g., \$20/11 calls)} \qquad (7.2)$$

$$\text{Efficiency} = (\text{Average cost per call})^{-1} \qquad (7.3)$$

Third, since changes in efficiency have no direct effect on cash, they are meaningless when used as a cash flow basis for justifying improvements. Many may try to argue that by being more efficient, getting 11 calls versus 10, there is a cost savings of, in this case, $0.18 cents per call. If so, how is the savings manifested as cash?

The conclusion is, being efficient does not improve your cash flow situation directly. Being more efficient only means you get more output from a given level of input. This is still a good thing. Many also reply to this statement saying, "Well, it may not be a cost reduction but if I'm more efficient, I can sell more!" Well, not so fast. First, most capacity in an organization has nothing to do with improved revenue. An efficient accounts payable clerk does not increase revenue, just as efficient HR data entry clerk doesn't affect revenue. From a manufacturing perspective, let's say more efficient production allows you to make more salable products. By being more efficient, you can make 20 products in the same time it used to take you to make 15. What if there were demand only for 15? What is the benefit of making more than there is demand for?

There's a disconnect between what accounting tells you is happening with efficiency and what is happening from a cash flow perspective. Efficiency does not lower your cost_C, but it does do something else for you. The keen reader will notice I have repeatedly suggested these have no direct cash implications. There are indirect ones however. I will demonstrate, in Chapter 17, the idea that efficiency alone does not lower your costs, but it does enable you to increase costs more slowly when expanding and to reduce them more quickly when reducing the size of your organization.

CHAPTER 8

Inventory

Inventory plays a key role when calculating profit, specifically gross profit. However, the dynamics related to inventory can be substantially incorrect from a cash flow perspective. For companies that make and sell inventory, this difference between what is represented on the income statement and what truly happens with cash can be significant. Inventory generally goes onto the profit and loss statement only when it is sold.[1] However, this can be very different, time wise, from when money was spent creating it.

There are three types of inventory: raw materials, work-in-process, and finished goods. Raw materials are the basic products and materials companies will buy anticipating converting them into salable products. This process of converting raw materials to finished product likely involves several steps. Think of a car being assembled. There are several steps required to put the car together, adding wheels to the chassis, body to the chassis, doors and windows to the body, and so on. Each process involves the consumption of capacity, and along with it, a cost is calculated. This value is $cost_{NC}$.

This calculated value is important to understand. Inventory is an asset from an accounting perspective. As it is transformed from raw materials to becoming a soon-to-be-finished product, the cumulative value of the effort must be tracked to determine the value of the asset for reporting purposes. A car that arrives at a door station in a production line has less financial value as an asset than when it leaves the station after people and machines do their work to add doors to it. Unfinished inventory is considered work-in-process inventory, or WIP. The value of WIP increases

---

[1]Accrual accounting rules suggest costs must be matched to when the revenues are recognized. If you build something today and sell it next year, the costs from the item built will show up when you sell the product next year.

throughout production until it reaches its maximum value as a finished good. At this point, no more work can be done, and it is ready to be sold. It is now a finished good to the company, and for reporting purposes. The calculated value of inventory throughout its steps can be represented in a chart, something like the one in Exhibit 8.1.

When you take a step back and think about it, money was spent building the inventory (Exhibit 8.2). From buying materials to buying

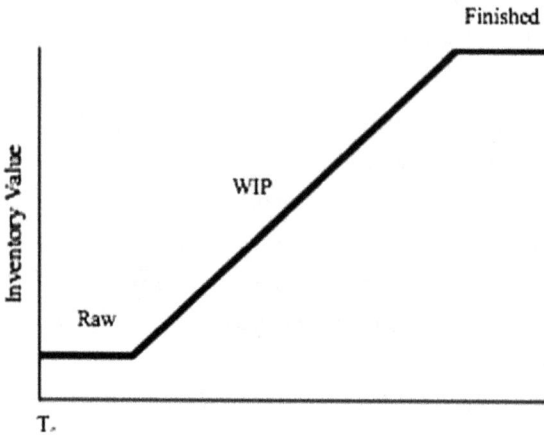

Exhibit 8.1 In the beginning T_0 inverntory value is primarily the value of the raw materials. As items are processed, the value of inventory, now work-in-process, increases to point where it reaches its maximum value as a finished product

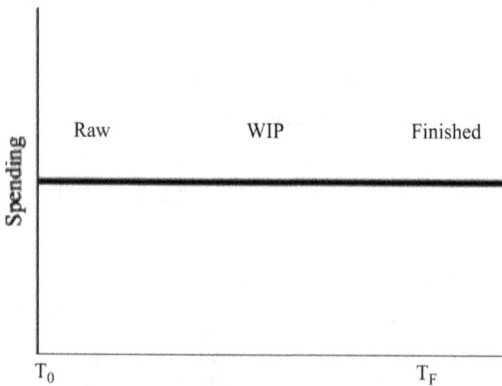

Exhibit 8.2 You are spending money throughout the process of building inventory. You are paying leases, paying for labor, buying materials, and so on. This money does not make it on to the income statement until the inventory is sold

the capacity used to increase the value at each step of the manufacturing process, money was spent. However, the money spent building inventory isn't captured on the profit and loss statement until the product is sold. Once sold, the value is taken off the balance sheet and put onto the profit and loss as a cost of the good that was sold. Even this value, however, isn't $cost_C$; it is $cost_{NC}$ because this represents the consumption of what you had previously bought.

Let's rephrase. We spend money building inventory, and this money spent goes into the value of the inventory. When the product is finished, it is ready to be sold. The time between when it becomes a finished product and when it is sold may or may not be known. However, we know we spent money making it, and this money doesn't show up on the income statement until the product is sold (Exhibit 8.3). Even when sold, it is $cost_{NC}$ not $cost_C$. This may be okay from a cash flow perspective when the items are purchased and the product is built and sold in the same analysis period. Otherwise, cash spent building an item at the end of one period and sold in a subsequent period means cash is affected while building the items in a completely different analysis period from when the profit calculation occurs. This creates a difference between what was spent and what is calculated as your profit.

This disconnect is troubling for many companies. They may show profit on their income statement, but they're confused about why they do not have any money. For many companies, especially small businesses, their money was spent building inventory that was not used to generate revenues. If there were a direct connection between cash flow and profit, this would not happen. But it does.

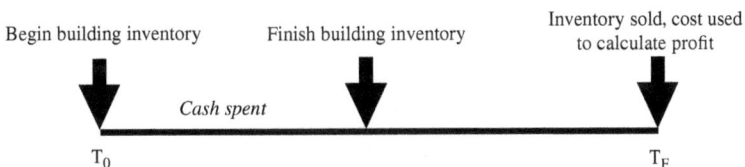

Exhibit 8.3 *The lag between when you spend money building inventory and when you receive payment for sold inventory can sometimes be significant. This would lead to situations where cash spent today may not be recognized as profit for many months if not years*

CHAPTER 9

Depreciation

Depreciation is another idea that does not seem to be considered holistically from a cash flow perspective when calculating profit. As a result, it fails to provide proper cash flow information when considering the transactions that involve depreciation. Let's say you buy a piece of equipment for $100,000, and let's assume you pay cash for it. You will now be $100,000 poorer from a cash flow perspective. This $100,000, however, doesn't make it to the income statement as a $100,000 cash transaction even though that is how you paid for it.

From an accounting perspective, that asset you purchased must now be depreciated. Let's say the equipment is depreciated equally over five years at $20,000 per year. The $20,000 goes onto the income statement and is involved in calculating profit. This creates an interesting scenario. First, the $20,000 has nothing to do with how you paid for the equipment. Second, and even more troubling, is that depreciation is considered a non-cash entry. This makes sense from the standpoint of it being an arbitrary number, but it also should represent what you paid for the equipment if profit truly represents cash flow. You are out $100,000 and that number does not show up as such on the income statement.

As a result of all this, with anything you buy that is depreciated, there'll be a difference, sometimes a significant difference, between the cash used in the transaction and how it is reported on the income statement. This issue can be manifested in several ways. The first is when you pay cash at one time and depreciation takes place over a longer time. It also happens when you're paying for the objects over time. The timing of the payments will be different from the depreciation schedule (Exhibit 9.1). You may pay off a loan in four or six years but have a five-year depreciation schedule. Finally, there may be a difference between the payment schedule and

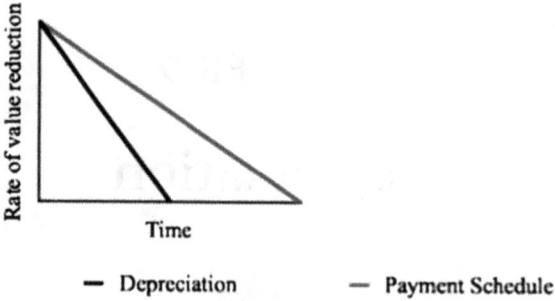

— Depreciation   — Payment Schedule

Exhibit 9.1 Your income statement sees your depreciation schedule. This rate can be very different from the cash you use to pay off any money you may owe

the dollar values for depreciation. The amount that you pay based on the terms of the loan may be very different from the dollar values that are used on the income statement,

Depreciation enters into profit your profit calculations, but it is not based on your cash flow dynamics; it is determined by the choice and application of an accounting rule, so it becomes another source of why profit isn't an effective proxy for cash flow.

PART 2

CHAPTER 10

Revisiting the Objective— Cash and Decision-Making

There comes a point when you have to ask the question, "What is my objective?" when it comes to financial decision-making. Companies spend an inordinate amount of time creating, analyzing, and trying to affect accounting data. They make substantial investments in large departments with many people, and in IT systems that sometimes seem almost singularly focused on creating and keeping track of accounting data. Consultants have made many billions, if not trillions, of dollars helping companies to cost better, calculate better cost data, and reduce their costs.

When you look at each of the cost accounting approaches that exist, what the people who designed them and use them fail to see is that it is the paradigm that is wrong, not the technique they use. Let me explain.

At the risk of alienating an industry for the sake of example, let's pick a simple concept. Let's say that you like to spend time spinning in circles to help you feel better, and you choose to do so, arbitrarily, in an anticlockwise manner. Your physician comes to you and says, "That doesn't work. It isn't going to help you feel better." So you decide to start spinning clockwise because you believe, and know in your heart, spinning does make a difference Things aren't better. You're still spinning. So you decide to do forward rolls. Again nice idea, but you're still spinning. You're just doing it around a different axis. The issue is, you're still trying to find a different or better way to spin, but the answer is: Spinning doesn't address the issue—no spinning does. Just because you create better or different way to spin doesn't mean you have solved your problem or have a better solution.

The same issue occurs with cost accounting. I was once a part of a discussion among cost accountants that was focused on trying to increase the relevance of their profession and of cost accounting in general. My suggestion to them? Stop costing. It doesn't matter how you choose to cost things. What is wrong is the notion of costing itself. There are three reasons costing is a bad practice, and it doesn't matter what technique you use:

1. To get a cost, you have to create and force math and relationships that do not exist.
2. By doing this, you lose touch with your operations.
3. You create meaningless numbers that people consider as gospel.

Forced Relationships

Remember the example of old telephone charges described in Chapter 6? The idea of land lines and long-distance calling charges? The question still remains: How do you determine the cost of a local call? You have to create an artificial relationship because a mathematical one does not exist. You can take the total number of calls and divide them into $25. You can consider the length of the call. You can even consider the number of ducks that fly over your building during the call. You can actually do anything because in the end, the relationship is arbitrary. It does not exist naturally or mathematically. The number of calls you make, the length of your calls, and the number of ducks have nothing to do with the $25 you pay per month.

The different costing approaches focus on helping you do the equivalent of determining how to assign the monthly fee to a local call. Each tries to come up with a better way to assign the costs, but in the end, they are still *spinning*. The issue isn't how you allocate cost or assign costs. It's *that* you're assigning them that makes it wrong.

Losing Track of Relationships

When you choose to create a relationship that does not exist, you lose information. Let's say you take the number of calls and divide them into the $25 fee you pay for service. If you make 25 calls, each call is calculated to cost you $1. How long was each call? Will the cost per call tell you? No. You don't know. Let's say next month the cost per call goes down to $0.96. What is that telling you? Does this mean you saved $0.04? How did you save it, and where is the four cents showing up each time you make a call? If it doesn't mean this, what does it mean?

In the latter example, you may have made one more phone call in the second month. You made 26 calls versus 25 calls. But when I tell you $1 per call versus $0.96 per call, although you may be able to back into the answer in this simple example, many situations are much more complicated. If you are making mobile phones, will you be able to tell, simply and clearly, where that four cents came from without detailed explanation? No. Additionally, in the case of the phone calls, which description made it easier to comprehend what actually happened? I made one more call or I saved $0.04? What does it mean when you reduce $cost_{NC}$ from $1 to $0.96? Regardless of what your answer is, we know it doesn't mean you save cash by making 26 calls because the cost for access is still $25.

With costing, you choose to go down an allocation path when you choose the technique you will use. Once you go down this path, the result is a single representation of an artificial reality. Assume you allocate costs using activity-based costing, and you end up with a number—a $cost_{NC}$. Now, let's assume you don't know how you got the cost, but you have it. Someone tells you it costs $12 to make an insulated mug. What do you know about what it took to create that mug either operationally or financially? Let's assume you try to reverse this process in its entirety without understanding how you got there. You will not have a complete picture of how you got to where you are cost wise. For example, if you use standard costing to calculate a cost savings, but the cost was calculated using activity-based allocations, your savings projections will likely be wrong because the assumptions used to get the $12 are very different from the assumptions you're using for improvements.

Meaningless Numbers

In the end, your cost per call is a meaningless number from a cash flow perspective. It is $cost_{NC}$. In addition, it can, in many situations, create the disconnect between accounting/finance and operations. What happens? Someone uses an approach, calculates a number, and now it's gospel. How many times have you heard someone talk about the cost to create an invoice or cut a check? No matter what attempts people make to explain why the number isn't valid, others have already latched on to it. Once they see this value, it now becomes the basis of conversation, regardless of how the number came to be.

Once on LinkedIn, a commenter decided to calculate a cost per meeting and wrote an article about it. Once mentioned, people accepted the number and discussed the implications, but *no one challenged the number*. How did this number come to be, and what does it mean? The author took salaries, created an hourly rate, and used that to determine the cost for the meeting. Let's say this cost was $1,000. Is your organization paying someone $1,000 to have a meeting? No. It is $cost_{NC}$. However, instead of asking whether this number had any relevance, everyone followed the first lemming off the cliff assuming this was an important and valid number, and committed themselves to it.[1] It wasn't valid. It meant nothing from a cash flow perspective, only from a $cost_{NC}$ perspective, and since many don't know the difference, they think paying $1000 for folks to have a meeting would be the same as paying someone $1,000 to come in and sit in a meeting room.

When people quote a *cost per* number, others latch onto it. It costs us $100 an invoice. Each customer service call is $6.75. These are $cost_{NC}$ values, but people often use them as if they were as good as gold. The reality is that most of the time, you don't spend any differently when you do work, suggesting $cost_C$ doesn't change. Recall, you pay to have the local phone service, so there is no $cost_C$ change when making local phone calls. The numbers are not real, but people hold on to them. They believe they are in the real world, but in reality, they are in the accounting equivalent of The Matrix and its subsequent artificial reality.

---

[1] I've heard the lemmings suicide story was false and was a story perpetuated by Disney. I'm ok with that because A. We are aware of the story and it works in this context, and B. How is this different from perpetuating a false story of a mouse being able to talk and carry on conversations?

The implications of these suggestions are huge. How much time and effort does your organization put into calculating these costs that are not related to cash? Likely lots, because they are hard to create and manage. They are all based on the approach you used to create them. Your systems have to be designed to reflect this approach. Your people have to identify variances and why they believe these non-cash costs may be increasing or decreasing. How much money does your organization spend trying to do what is mathematically the equivalent of trying to calculate, manage, and reduce the cost of a local call? My guess is, a lot. These numbers they are managing are assumed to be the equivalent of cash. They aren't. Companies spend millions of dollars on people and information technology to manage costs that have nothing to do with money. What decisions are being affected by this information? You decided to make a huge investment in technology or lean because you will save $10 million. What if $9.5 million were cost$_{NC}$ and only $0.5 were true cash savings, cost$_C$? Would it change the decisions you make? It should. How you calculate the ROI? If you spend $2 million, your cash flow ROI will not be 4:1. Instead, it will be –0.75:1. Isn't this difference pretty significant?

What is your objective? Is it to create numbers that you know are wrong for the sake of having a number? Or is the objective to understand your organization and to make better decisions as a result so you can improve cash flow? To understand how some things you do will not affect cash at all, and to be able to identify them and plan for them?

The bottom line is this. You may be thinking the same thing as many others have asked me; I understand what you are saying, but at least I have something when I have a cost!" My response is, why is having a useless number better? Think about these three characteristics of costs.

1. There is no single cost
2. Costs are created through arbitrary relationships
3. Costs are not tied to cash flow

No Single Cost

The cost you have is determined by the approach you use. The calculated costs using different methods do not converge to a single value as you would expect or hope it would if there were just one cost. Ten thermometers

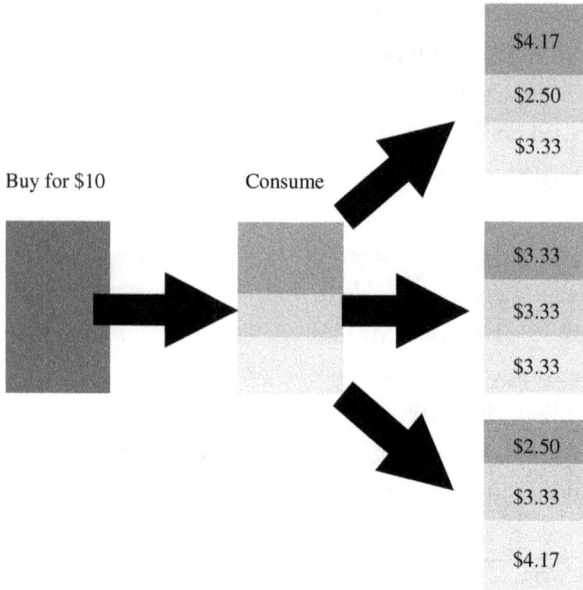

Multiple descriptions of costs

Exhibit 10.1 Even though you bought something and consumed it one way, it is possible to create multiple representations of what that consumption costs

might create confidence that the temperature is a single number say 55°F. This should tell you that each measurement device, considering the inherent error, will still come up with a value that represents the reality of the environment. The same does not happen when calculating costs—determining a value for $cost_{NC}$. Each approach takes the same information and creates a unique value, which should cause you to question any value you get at all (Exhibit 10.1)

Arbitrary Relationships

As stated throughout the early parts of this chapter, the dynamics of calculating $cost_{NC}$ require arbitrary relationships to be created. When you pay someone a salary and you want to calculate the cost of a report she creates, there is no relationship between her salary and what she does or creates, including the report you're trying to cost. As mentioned before, the only way to make a connection is to make one up.

Because this relationship is arbitrary, its inherent value should be called into question.

No Ties to Cash Flow

As stated numerous times previously, calculated costs, $cost_{NC}$, have no relationship with cash flow. You can lower $cost_{NC}$ and have no effect on cash. For example, if costs per call were calculated by dividing the number of calls into the $25, making more calls has no effect on cash, yet $cost_{NC}$ is lower. Likewise, you can reduce cost and have no effect on profitability. If you lower the cost of a meeting to $500 by cutting a $1,000 meeting in half time-wise, not only does it not affect cash flow, it would not affect profit either, since sales, general, and administrative (SGA) numbers on your income statement will not change just because you're efficient. SGA costs are mostly tied to what you buy, not how you use it.

In the end, what are you trying to accomplish? Ultimately, I would propose that the objective of all this is to put yourself in a position to understand how you spend your money, what you buy, and how to get desired output levels in an efficient and productive manner. You want to make decisions that will help you improve cash flow and avoid promising improvements from investments that ultimately fall flat. If you can do this, you should be in a good position, and the fact is, you can do this without calculating cost and without using accounting data.

The hypothesis that shapes the rest of this book is that you can get information you're looking for without a single $cost_{NC}$ being calculated. The idea is to look at how your company is structured, what it buys, and how efficiently it creates output. This will provide you with simple understandable data that not only helps you see your organization more clearly, but you'll also have much more correct and relevant data than you would have using the output from cost accounting. What is this approach? Understanding and managing capacity. Let's begin by creating a foundation.

CHAPTER 11

Transactions and Capacity

When I was getting my PhD in engineering, my previous experiences and studies suggested that it would be important for me to be able to explain any ideas I created from an engineering perspective to financial types, and to do so in their language. This led to my initial studies in accounting.

As I learned accounting techniques, many things did not make sense to me. Why do costs go down as I create more output? Why isn't there just one cost that represents the creation of a product or the execution of a process or service? I began by looking at things—profit, costs, cash flow—from an engineering perspective. Borrowing ideas from thermodynamics, fluid mechanics, and system dynamics, I created a model that I thought should represent costs, profit, and accounting data. I thought the model was quite sound, but accounting predicted quite different results.

The big difference was how costs were handled. The model I created was based on the assumption that costs represent cash flow—money leaving a company as expressed simply in Exhibit 11.1. I found this was not true, so I sought to correct this for my own analysis purposes.

With the model I developed, costs *were* defined as money leaving the company. According to this definition, money leaves the company because I paid for something, and only when I pay for something. If this is

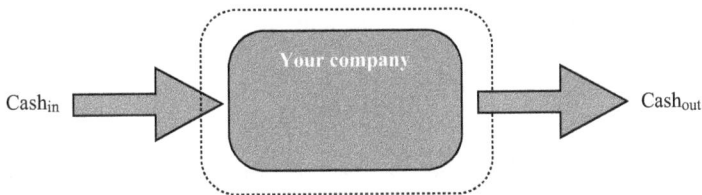

Exhibit 11.1 *This model represents the simple flow of cash. Anything that comes in is cash revenue, Revenue$_C$, and what leaves is cost$_C$. The difference is the cash profit*

the case, money leaves only when there is a financial transaction involving a cash payment. There are three types of transactions:

1. Buying capacity
2. One-off scenarios
3. Obligations

Capacity

Capacity represents the largest expenditure for almost all businesses. I define capacity as what you buy in anticipation of demand or use. This includes space, labor, materials, most information technology, and equipment. When you step back to think about it, this financial number is significant. It is also the cost that costing approaches seek to allocate or assign. Think about this for a minute. Accounting significantly skews the understanding and management of your largest expenditure.

One-off Scenarios

One-offs represent activities when one buys goods or services once. The one-off represents a clearly identifiable transfer of goods or services for cash. An easy way to compare the differences between capacity and one-offs would be to consider a situation where you have a grounds crew to take care of landscaping versus hiring someone from the outside. You buy landscaping equipment, storage space, and landscaping employees in anticipation of using them. Regardless of whether you use what you buy or not, you pay to have them. This is capacity. A one-off would be having a company come in, and you pay them to perform landscaping services. Similarly, capacity would be your ability to make local phone calls. One-off would be an individual long-distance call.

Obligations

Obligations are simply transactions that involve an exchange of cash, but not for a good or service—something you are obligated to pay. An example would be paying taxes. You're obligated, by law, to pay taxes based on earnings.

The purpose of the three descriptions is to help you understand that transactions buy different things for different purposes. Consider the phone calls example. Local service would be like buying capacity. You pay to have it to use. Long-distance calls are one-offs, each being determined by the attributes of a specific call. You are obligated to pay the large taxes on your bill based on your use.

With one-offs, since there is a clear relationship between $cost_C$ and what was purchased, there is rarely ambiguity. With capacity, however, there is ambiguity when calculating $cost_{NC}$ because of the arbitrary relationships required. Because capacity is the largest expenditure and because you cannot create a direct cost relationship that isn't arbitrary between the capacity you buy and what you create from it, I will focus the rest of the book on helping you understand capacity, how to assess its use, and how to manage it.

CHAPTER 12

Input Capacity

When John Wiley & Sons ask me to write *Essentials of Capacity Management*, my first thought was, "Who would want to read a book about capacity?" I had written *Explicit Cost Dynamics* to create a mathematical and philosophical basis for cash flow models and other concepts I subsequently developed and am sharing with you in this book. *Explicit Cost Dynamics* had, what I perceived to be, a hole in my explanation of the mathematical model. I compare this hole to dark matter with physics. For a long time, physicists said it was there, that the math supported it, but they struggled proving it. The math told me there was something there. I hadn't defined it clearly, but the math was very clear and suggesting it was there. In the book, I called this black box "resources."

As I began to write *Essentials*, I realized these resources were just capacity. I began to define capacity as all things purchased in anticipation of use. This includes space, labor, materials, equipment, and information technology, what I called capacity entities. Over time, however, I began to think there was more than one type of capacity; that the five "entities" mentioned in *Essentials* did not tell the whole story. When you have someone for eight hours, that time and that cost are fixed. However, what is created during that eight hours may vary. One person may have different output levels on different days, just as two people can have different outputs levels on the same day. This led to the creation of and distinction between input capacity and output capacity. Capacity, as defined in *Essentials*, transformed into input capacity, and output was defined subsequently as what input creates. This is described in the next chapter.

I sometimes refer to input capacity as static capacity.[1] The term represents the transaction associated with buying the capacity that you hope to use—what you are truly paying for in anticipation of use. There are a few key attributes of input capacity:

1. There is a cash transaction involved.
2. What you pay is determined by how much you buy and the price you pay for the amount you bought.
3. The cost is independent of how it is used.

Cash Transactions

With the various types of input capacity, space, labor, equipment, information technology, and materials, you pay for what you have. The terms of payment may vary, of course, but the fact remains that there is a transfer of money to have the capacity available for your use.

Cost Determined by What is Purchased

The second common attribute of input capacity is that you pay based on how much you buy. If you lease 10,000 ft² of office space, the price for that is determined and agreed upon, and you get the 10,000 ft². Similarly, if you buy 500 linear feet of paper or one week of someone's time, there is a single price for that single amount purchased.

The only way the cost of capacity changes for you is when you buy a different amount of capacity, you buy it at a different price, or both. This is shown in Exhibit 12.1.

The Cost is Independent of Use

In math, two things are independent when a dependent variable, what is on the vertical or Y-axis, does not change with the independent

---

[1] In the early stages of developing these ideas, static was chosen because attributes such as price and quantity did not change. Later, I realized that this static capacity was the same as input to a process – what I start with or use to create output, hence the name input. I use both in conversation depending on the context.

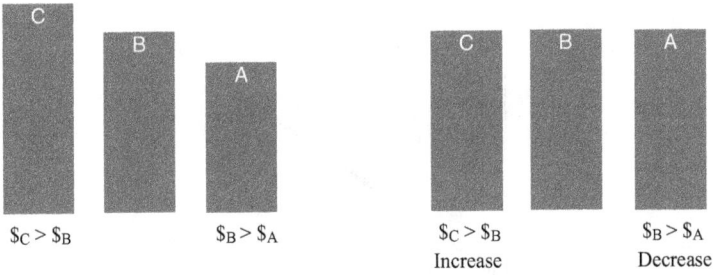

Exhibit 12.1 It is important to understand how cost$_C$ changes with capacity. To reduce costs, you must either buy less or buy cheaper. Think about buying gas. The less you buy at once or the cheaper the price, the lower the cost for that transaction. In this Exhibit, on the left, you can see that the more you buy, the more you will spend. On the right, when you can buy the same amount of capacity at a cheaper price, you can reduce cost$_C$

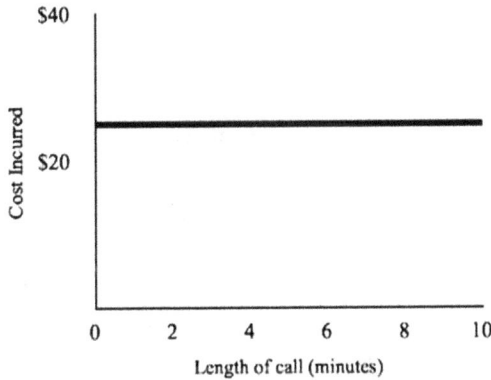

Exhibit 12.2 There is no change to the cost incurred for local service based on call length. This suggests there is no relationship between the two. They are mathematically independent

variable, what is on the horizontal or X-axis. This can be represented as a straight horizontal line (Exhibit 12.2). For example, with long-distance calls, the price depended on time. Time is independent; it is whatever it is. However, price depends on how long the call was. There is a direct relationship between the cost and how long the call was, as shown in Exhibit 12.3.

However, with input capacity, there is no direct relationship between cost and use. How much you pay for space is determined by how

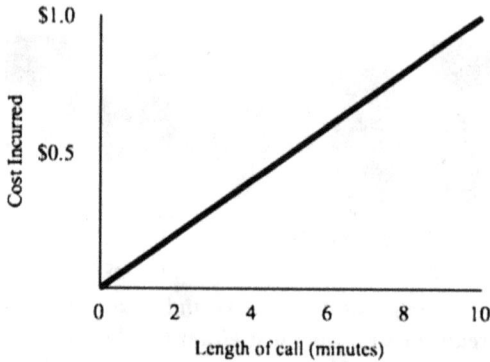

Exhibit 12.3 *Unlike local calls, there is a direct relationship between the cost you incur and the amount of time you speak. The reason is simple. When you buy minutes, the more minutes you buy, the more expensive it is for you. With local calls, you aren't buying minutes, hence the lack of a change*

much you bought and not what you choose to do with it, as shown in Exhibits 12.4 and 12.5.

These attributes of input capacity are critical to understand. It is for these reasons that accounting struggles to create a cost for output. All calculated costs, costs$_{NC}$, have to be created by assigning capacity costs to

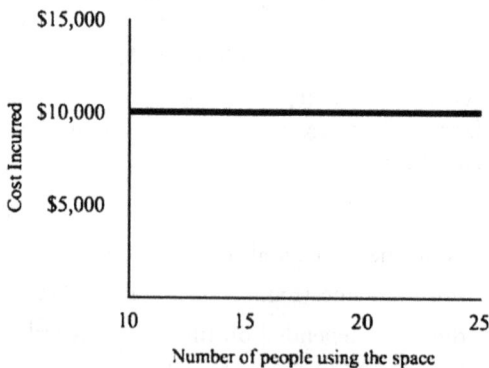

Exhibit 12.4 *Notice how input capacity behaves the same way as access to local phone service. The number of people using the space does not affect what is paid for the space. Hence, to calculate a cost per person would require a relationship that does not exist*

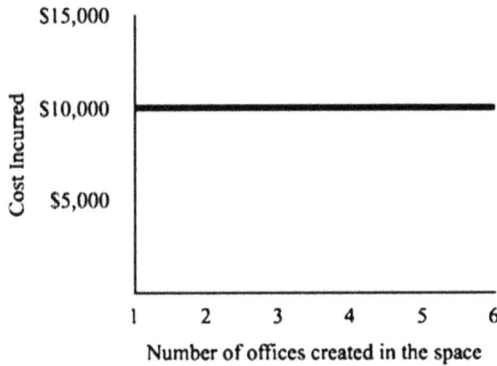

Exhibit 12.5 Similar to Exhibit 12.4, the number of offices or, abstractly, the number of anything that represents the use of space has no effect on cost. Hence, the idea about being space efficient and using space more effectively does not, itself, affect cash

what you create from it. This is because there is no mathematical relationship between what you buy, input capacity, and how it is used. Recall, the lack of a relationship between local service and the cost of a phone call. More on this later. Now, on to output capacity.

CHAPTER 13

Output Capacity

The notion of output capacity came after *Essentials,* because I had not yet separated the two logically. I thought capacity was capacity. I was wrong.

When you buy input capacity, you can use it to do work. Space can accommodate offices and production lines. People can hire others, serve others, design, make, and do things. Materials can be used to perform work or be used in the conversion process of manufacturing products. When you buy input capacity, the output capacity or what you can create from the input, can be affected by many factors, such as knowledge and skill sets. Two people who work the same eight-hour shift will have different levels of output. Other factors affect output as well. Policies and procedures can limit how much output one can create. How efficient or inefficient a process is, too, can influence how much output is created.

It is by understanding output capacity that you can begin to understand why accounting fails and why you need surrogate information to get your arms around operational and financial data. There are two very important attributes of output capacity:

1. Output capacity consumes input capacity.
2. There is no cost transaction involved when output capacity consumes input capacity.

Consuming Input

When you buy input capacity, you are buying something you expect to turn into work or to be consumed in the creation of work and work products. Creating work, therefore, consumes the input. Let's assume you have a worker who creates reports. You buy them for eight hours. If each report takes an hour to create, one hour is consumed of the eight hours you bought with each report.

There is No Cash Transaction

When you consume input capacity, there is no cash transaction involved. Remember, you purchased the input capacity and you have it for use. This is a $cost_C$ transaction. The employee making reports doesn't create a cash transaction with each report. The cash is tied to the fact that they're there and available to you to do the work that you need.

This is a key reason accounting fails. The primary focus of costing is to put a dollar value on output—the consumption of input. It attempts to do this by force-fitting a relationship between input capacity and output capacity that does not exist. However, when you consider the attributes of both the input and output capacity, it becomes clear this cannot happen.

The next chapter will begin to consider the relationship between input capacity and output capacity, which becomes the basis of the information you'll need to manage more effectively.

CHAPTER 14

Understanding the Basics of Capacity Dynamics

When you look at your organization from capacity perspective, you begin to see common activities differently and more clearly. This chapter will explain the basic concepts of capacity dynamics and how they affect, or are affected by, everyday activities and your company.

As I suggested in Chapter 12, you buy input capacity in finite amounts. This finite amount will be represented throughout the rest of this book by a rectangle as seen in Exhibit 14.1.

The height of the rectangle will represent the amount of capacity you purchase. As seen in Exhibit 14.2, different input capacity scenarios can be represented this way.

As you begin to consume the capacity by creating output, less of it is available. For instance, if you have someone for eight hours and two hours are spent in meetings, you now have only six hours to use. Once you begin using the 10,000 ft² of office space that you lease, the used space is no longer available for something else (Exhibit 14.3).

There are two important issues to consider when trying to understand this relationship. First, note, if you're considering an analysis period, once the period is complete, the capacity transactions have been defined and the descriptions of what happens during the period are unambiguous.

Exhibit 14.1 The rectangle will represent input capacity. It represents what you buy and what you now have access to. It is both a financial representation and an operational representation

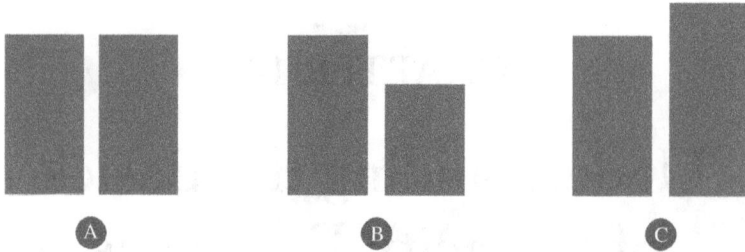

Exhibit 14.2 *Since the rectangles can represent both financial values and operational values, it is important to both keep them and consider them in the same context. Financially, A would be capacity that costs the same, with B and C reflecting the rectangle on the right having lower and higher cost$_C$, respectively. Operationally, A represents the same amount of capacity with B and C representing situations where there is either less capacity or more capacity*

Exhibit 14.3 *The lighter colored rectangles represent the consumption or use of capacity. Once the initially available capacity is consumed, less of it is available. Note, when considered in the financial sense, the value of the capacity has not changed when consumed*

The work you did last month and the efficiency with which you did it can no longer be changed. There's only one way to describe that analysis period from an activity perspective. Second, when you're planning, you can think about and often project the input capacity you have and how work will consume this capacity. This positions you to understand the rate at which capacity is being consumed and, therefore, to predict when you have to make investments in more capacity. These investments affect cash flow. Consider the following example.

Assume a company sells space. Every time a sales transaction takes place, a finite amount of the space is used. You calculate a cost$_{NC}$ associated with the transaction. Consumption of the space has no financial effect. However, what happens if you are out of capacity and you have another sale? Now you're obligated to buy more input capacity although the $cost_{NC}$, once the capacity is available, will remain the same. Knowing how much capacity you have and how much is available makes capacity planning and, therefore, cash flow planning much simpler. Accounting would not have predicted the need to spend more money on capacity, therefore affecting cash flow because accounting doesn't model capacity and capacity utilization.

When you consider the purchase and use of capacity, you will clearly want to understand how efficiently and productively you're using it. It is your biggest $cost_C$ category, so managing it becomes critically important. Let's look at how this works.

When you buy input, there are three states in which it can exist:

1. Productive work—creating output for which there is need or demand
2. Unproductive work—creating output for which there is no need or demand
3. Idle—creating no output

The objective for most operational improvement activities is, or should be, to increase the efficiency of productive capacity, to get more productive output for the same input. Sometimes, however, unproductive capacity gets in the way. Doing unnecessary work may limit your ability to do productive work. If you have a sales person, for example, and you have them spend an inordinate amount of time filling out reports that have limited value or are rarely used, the reports consume available input capacity that could otherwise be used for productive work; selling. If the reports aren't helping them sell more, and if generating the reports is taking time away from selling, this may be considered unproductive from a sales perspective, and this lost time cannot be recovered.

As mentioned previously, approaches to improving performance and reducing $cost_C$ and $cost_{NC}$ focus on improving the amount of productive capacity and minimizing unproductive capacity. Process improvement, lean, Six Sigma, and information technology all profess to focus on improving productive work. They look to simplify tasks, eliminate unproductive activities, and make it easier to get more from the same or less input. Unproductive work and, in some cases, idle time, are the fat that lean tries to eliminate. However, if the capacity states are not identified explicitly, it is possible to improve the rate of unproductive work. For instance, consider suggestions to overbuild in the name of being efficient. Processes focused on reducing $cost_{NC}$ may encourage more work to be done than necessary, which is unproductive. This is covered in more detail in Chapter 15.

I'd like to shift gears and focus on three key aspects of capacity dynamics that will help you see, understand and manage capacity more effectively. These are efficiency, effectiveness, and productivity.

Efficiency

As discussed in Chapter 7, efficiency is the ratio of output to input. In capacity terms, it is the ratio of output capacity to input capacity, or of dynamic capacity to static capacity. As you can see in Exhibit 14.4, increases in efficiency can happen under either or a combination of the two options. It is the same principle at work when considering miles per gallon with your car. You start with a gallon and the question is: How far can you drive with that gallon? More efficient vehicles drive farther on a gallon, of course, than less-efficient vehicles. The other method is to go the same distance using less fuel. Both are improvements in efficiency.

There is another idea I'd like to share while we're on this topic. The price you pay for capacity, too, is an input, and so in this context, the amount of gas you buy is the output. This allows you to factor in the cost of the capacity to calculate cost efficiencies. For example, compare buying gas at $4 per gallon versus $3.90. One way to look

Exhibit 14.4 *Increase in efficiency can happen one or both of two ways. With the same level of input, you create more output, as is seen in A. Second, you create the same level of output with less input, shown in B*

at it is, you received the same output, one gallon, for a lower price. Another way to consider is, for the same input, $4, you can get more output, gasoline.

Considering this, the efficiency discussion can now be opened up to miles driven at a given cost$_C$. Hence, driving 30 miles for $4 is more efficient than driving 15 miles for $4. This frees you to consider multiple options with dissimilar inputs. For instance, which is more efficient, 10 customer service calls for $20 or eight calls for $15? You can now begin considering the cost of capacity along with output to understand cost efficiency.

Effectiveness

Effectiveness considers the amount of capacity you *should* have versus how much you *do* have. When you buy something, you expect it to be available to you. When it is not, it affects how effective it can be for you. If a new person joins your group but spends half his time wrapping up responsibilities from the previous job, for instance, they are not available to you, so their effectiveness has been decreased.

As seen in Exhibit 14.5, effectiveness may affect your output capacity. In situations where your capacity is involved with creating productive work, a lack of available capacity limits how much productive work you may be able to achieve. In the end, it is as if you bought less input capacity for the same price. This approach is less cost-efficient. See Exhibit 14.6.

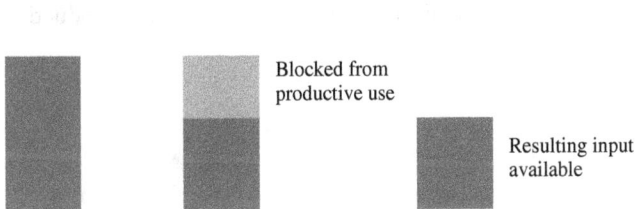

Blocked from productive use

Resulting input available

Exhibit 14.5 Poor effectiveness can be a capacity killer. Consider space with columns throughout, which limits how much can be used, or a delivery driver whose truck is down for repair. Unproductive meetings, too, can affect effectiveness. Effectiveness is often overlooked, leading to less output being created and, potentially, the need to buy more input

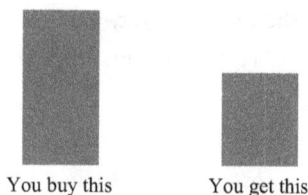

You buy this   You get this

Exhibit 14.6 You purchase the amount of capacity at a given price. However, activities that reduce effectiveness reduce the available amount of what you purchased. The result is seen in the rectangle on the right. Therefore, for the same price, you get what ends up being less input capacity. This leads to a lower cost efficiency

Productivity

Many look at productivity and consider it to be synonymous with efficiency. I tend to look at them differently. Although productivity can be the ratio of output to input, as is efficiency, I tend to take it one step further. Productivity should be focused on how efficiently I do work for which there is demand. Think about it this way. What does it matter if I am doing work that no one wants or needs? It is waste, no matter how efficiently I created it. This is why I draw the distinction.

Output should be aligned with the demand for it. Otherwise, you are consuming input unnecessarily (Exhibit 14.7). This can sometimes create the false perception that you need more input because the input you currently have is being consumed, although for unproductive work. You should know how much demand there is, whether you can or do meet it doing productive work, and how efficiently you did so. In Appendix B, I have described the math that helps explain the use of productivity and capacity metrics.

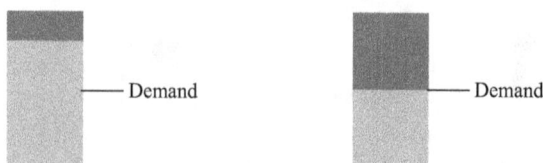

———— Demand   ———— Demand

Exhibit 14.7 On the left, you can see a situation where one may be very efficient, but unproductive. This happens when companies overly focus on lowering unit costs without considering how much demand there is for what they're making. On the right, you see a situation where there is little waste in terms of output, but there is clearly a situation where there is too much input capacity

CHAPTER 15

Understanding the Cost Dynamics of Capacity

When doing research, consulting, and just talking to people about capacity and costing, one thing that becomes clear is, there is a general lack of understanding of the interactions between allocated capacity costs and cash flow by the accounting community and those who use accounting tools. Much of this belief stems from the notion that to many of them, costs are costs, and they are all the same; there is no difference between $cost_C$ and $cost_{NC}$. Also, they believe both are generally cash numbers. Of course, we know this is not true. However, their need to create $cost_{NC}$ by costing work, products, and activities so they understand the so-called financial implications of products, services, and activities begins to validate this idea in their heads. The rest stems from a general lack of understanding of capacity types and dynamics. The idea of inputs and outputs, of what is static and what is dynamic, is not language they know, understand, or use. To understand companies the way they believe they do, however, they must understand capacity because of its influence on the cash dynamics of a company.

When we buy input, we are buying a static amount at a fixed price. This is the largest $cost_C$ component of most companies. We buy a day or a year of someone's time. We buy a certain amount of square feet, number of machines, pounds of material, or amount of terabytes. When you plot the cost to buy capacity, it looks like the graph in Exhibit 15.1. Notice two things. First, the $cost_C$ is tied to how much we buy. Second, the only way the value, $cost_C$, changes is if we change the amount or capacity we buy or the price at which we buy it (Exhibit 15.2).

Upon buying input capacity, we can use it to do work (Exhibit 15.3). Notice when we began consuming input capacity, there is no change to

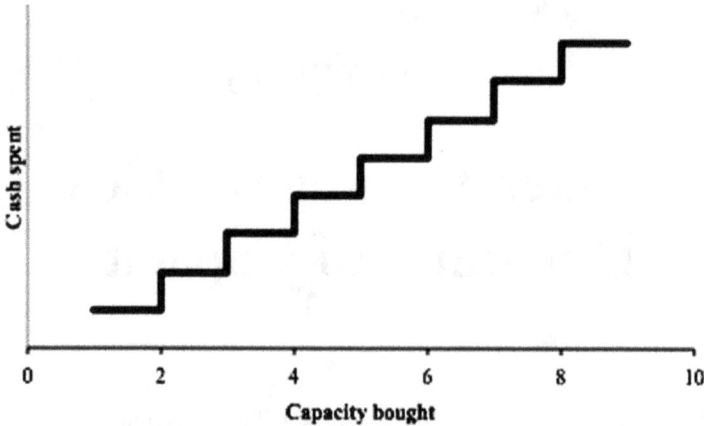

Exhibit 15.1 Capacity is no different from any other financial transaction. Capacity cost is tied to how much you buy and the price you pay. The only time capacity costs go up, therefore, is when you buy more capacity or the price that you buy has increased. This is why capacity costs and how you use capacity are mathematically independent

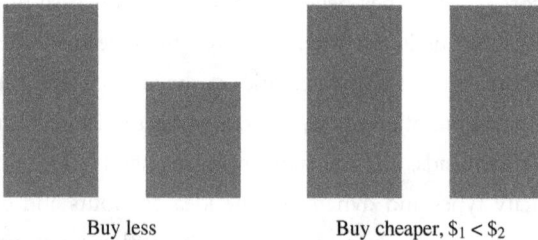

Buy less   Buy cheaper, $1 < $2

Exhibit 15.2 When buying input, there are only two ways to reduce costs: either buy less or buy the same thing cheaper. For instance, if you want to reduce space costs, you either have to reduce the total area you are buying, or find a location that offers the same amount of area at a lower price

what we paid for it. The cost$_C$ and the output are mathematically in-dependent, because no matter how we change the independent variable (output), the dependent variable (cost$_C$) does not change, as seen in Chapter 12 and repeated here for convenience in Exhibit 15.4.

Contrast this with buying labor based on output rather than time. If I pay you one dollar for each piece of output you create, you will see a direct relationship between output and cost$_C$. It's like long-distance

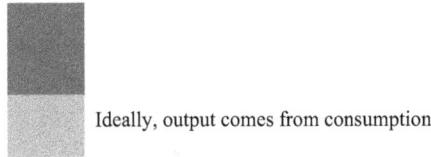

Ideally, output comes from consumption

Exhibit 15.3 You buy input capacity to have it available for consumption. Consuming input ideally creates output. However, the act of consumption, of creating output, does not change what you paid for your capacity

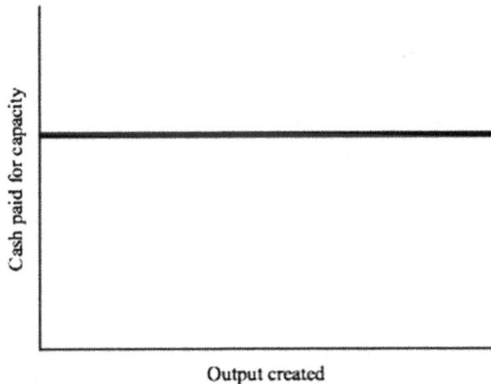

Exhibit 15.4 There is no mathematical relationship between the capacity you buy and what you do with it. Capacity costs change only when you buy more or higher-priced capacity. Because there is no relationship between output and capacity, and because cost accounting wants a relationship between the two, it must create artificial relationships

phone calls. That creates a scenario where the cash is tied directly to what is created, output, and the resulting chart looks like the one seen in Exhibit 15.5.

What if you want to calculate the cost of output created by your input capacity? You will find yourself needing to use a cost allocation technique, and if you do, you will find yourself in a precarious position. There is no mathematical relationship between the output and what you bought, but you need one to calculate costs. If you do not have one and you need one, you have to resort to arbitrary assignments to get your answer. You have no choice. Let me explain.

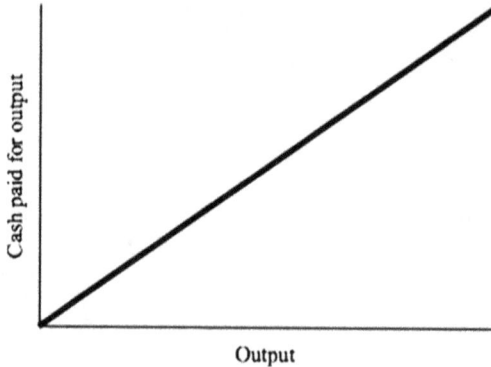

Exhibit 15.5 This chart is very similar to Exhibit 15.1 conceptually. This chart suggests the more output you buy, the more you have to pay for it. Exhibit 15.1 says: the more capacity you buy, the more you have to pay for it. This suggests that cost$_C$ changes only with what you buy

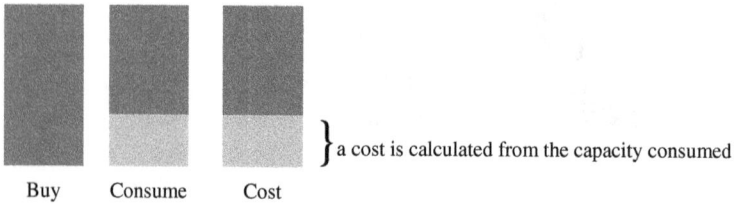

} a cost is calculated from the capacity consumed

Buy   Consume   Cost

Exhibit 15.6 Cost accounting attempts to put a financial value on consumed capacity. Since the values are independent and an arbitrary and artificial relationship must be created to calculate this value, we end up with a multitude of approaches trying to come up with the best way to determine this "cost." If a relationship already existed, one wouldn't need to create one

Let's say you want to calculate the cost of a customer service call. The anatomy of the situation can be seen in Exhibit 15.6. To get a cost for output (the call), you will need to allocate the input costs, the customer service rep's salary to the call. Either there could be logic behind it such as with purposeful allocations—using techniques such as activity-based costing—or you can do it by spreading costs using a less purposeful approach. Let's consider both.

Purposeful Allocation Techniques

Purposeful allocation involves attempting to use some sort of logic to assign capacity costs to output. Approaches such as activity based costing and standard costing set parameters that attempt to use logic or reason as a basis the allocation or assigning of costs. For example, if someone makes $30 per hour, one inclination may be to suggest that each minute costs $0.50. So 10-minute task would cost $5.

Although it may seem logical, this number is still not $cost_C$; hence, it has no cash implications. If you make another call, you will not see a charge for, and your cash change by five dollars. However, the costing numbers tell a different story. Let's say your $cost_{NC}$ for a 10-minute task is $5. This would suggest that if you could reduce this value by consuming less input or doing more tasks you can reduce costs, specifically, $cost_{NC}$, but believed to be $cost_C$ (Exhibit 15.7).

I'd like to take a moment to offer an example of believing $cost_{NC}$ is the same as $cost_C$ is a conversation I had with a health-care executive who suggested that a day in the hospital costs $7,000. The thought this person had was that if they could reduce the cumulative length of stays annually by 1,000 days, they could save $7 million. He believed that the $7,000 was cash.

This number was calculated primarily by allocating capacity costs to a patient day during a hospital visit. There is the cost of her room, carved out of what is paid for the building. There is the time the nurses and other staff spent with the patient. There are tests to be run, drugs to be

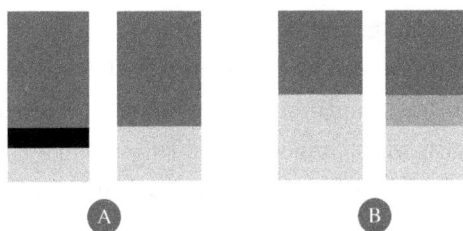

Exhibit 15.7 Cost_{NC} *can vary due to changes in capacity consumption rates. In A, we see a reduction in consumption equal to the amount in black. This would suggest that* cost_{NC} *has gone down. In B, the consumption has increased by the amount in medium grey suggesting a cost increase. Clearly, there are no changes to the capacity costs; hence,* cost_C *has not been affected by the improvements*

administered, and so on. The cash costs do not change based on whether a patient is there or not. The allocated costs are values placed on the consumption of resources when taking care of a patient for a day. This calculated value is the essence of cost$_{NC}$.

If you are the decision maker and you don't realize the $7 million is not real, you are duped into believing that there is a huge financial opportunity on the table. Instead of basking in the glory of making a $1 million investment to gain $7 million in improvements, you're left on the hook to explain to your boss or your board why you invested $1 million and barely broke even.

Changing how you consume capacity may affect cost$_{NC}$, as seen in Exhibit 15.7. You consume less, so it makes sense that something should go down. However, changing the rate of consumption of what you have already paid for does not change cash, it just improves your efficiency.

Less Purposeful

When costs are allocated without regard to whether there is a different rate of capacity consumption or some attempt to add purpose to the allocation, the cost assignment is less purposeful. One example is the average cost per unit. With the average cost per unit, you basically take your capacity cost and divide it by output. Pictorially, it is seen in Exhibit 15.8.

If someone made 30 calls in an hour where they made $30, each call had a calculated average cost of $1. If you made more calls, the average cost per call would be less than $1. If you made fewer than 30 calls, the average cost would be greater than $1.

There are many issues with this approach, of course. An assumption may be all calls have similar attributes. Although this may be okay in some cases such as when considering call length with a fairly small time standard deviation, what happens if there is a large standard deviation? One client used this broad approach to cost their products. The most simple product had the same cost$_{NC}$ as products that were many times more difficult and complex from a production perspective, with substantially more labor and material consumption. Again, both had the same cost$_{NC}$.

This created an issue for that client. The question was what to charge their clients when the costs don't reflect effort, complexity, and capacity

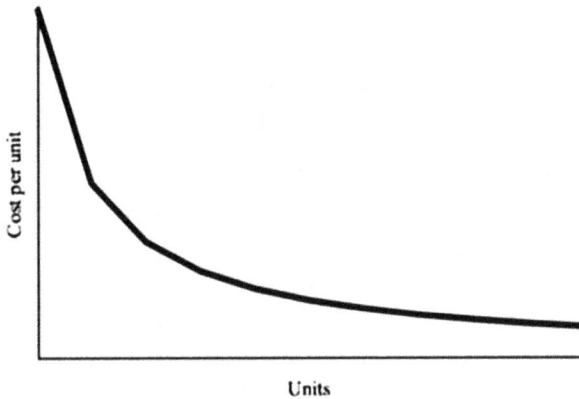

Units

Exhibit 15.8 When you take a capacity cost and divide it by output, you end up with the average cost hyperbola. The question must be asked, though: What does this curve tell you? We have established that cost per unit represents $cost_{NC}$ and, therefore, does not affect cash. Logically, considering Exhibit 15.1, the idea that the more you create, the more capacity you'd consume and, therefore, possibly buy, $cost_C$ should be a monotonically increasing function with respect to consumption. Simply, this means that as consumption rates increase, the cost of the capacity will either remain the same or increase. Consuming capacity will not put you in a position where the cost, $cost_C$, goes down with increased use. If $cost_C$ does not go down but this curve does over the same domain, how useful is this curve? It describes the opposite of reality

consumption? One answer is, of course, your effort doesn't matter when it comes to pricing. Have you ever purchased a car, a meal, or clothes at a given price solely because of the perceived effort of creating it? Rarely, if ever. Generally, you have no idea how much effort was put into the bottle of wine, the suit jacket, or the phone you just bought. Another answer is that cost, itself, is irrelevant when it comes to pricing.

We generally do not buy based on effort or cost; we buy based on the perception of value. However, by being smart, extra effort may be captured and articulated in ways that increase the perception of value. Hand-built cars and custom-tailored suits may be perceived as being more valuable; therefore, they often demand a higher price. Also, specialty items may consume more input, so this may limit your revenue potential unless you earn a higher price. In this client's case, the fact that they would take the time to create specialized products and packaging should increase the perception of value if marketed properly. In addition to not affecting cash flow, there is another reason modeling cost$_{NC}$ is of limited value: the same set of circumstances can create different costs. Let me explain as this issue also came up in Chapter 10.

There are many ways to calculate the cost of a customer service call. Each approach leads to its own answers, and if two answers converge, it is likely a coincidence. Exhibit 15.9 shows how the same scenario can create multiple answers; multiple costs. These different costs are due to the various ways of assigning input costs.

If one scenario leads to multiple costs, you have to ask, which cost is right? Is any one of them right? What does right mean in this context? I regularly deal with executives of companies who tell me they understand their costs very well. But do they? Since costing requires the arbitrary assignment of capacity, you, I, or anyone else could come along and create a different cost value in as much detail, from the same set of circumstances and data. So, although they may have precise information about their particular costing calculus, anyone else can come along and create a completely different and equally valid calculus that could challenge theirs.

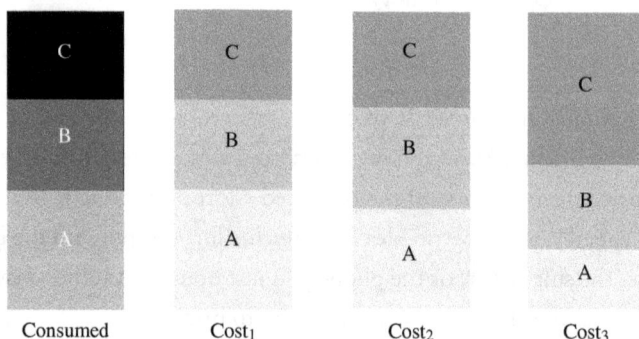

Exhibit 15.9 *In physics, there is an idea that you cannot know the exact location of an electron. The reason is the technique you would use to determine where the electron is would move the electron. It would be like your GPS moving you every time it tried to figure out where you are. Costing is similar. The answer you get when trying to calculate the cost changes with the technique you use and how you use it. Given this to be the case, how confident can you be with any calculated cost number?*

Conclusion

The cost dynamics of capacity are simple. You buy capacity and you pay for it. That's it. All the attempts of individuals, accounting groups, and organizations to come up with a better way to cost are just attempts to create a different way to allocate costs—to create relationships where they do not exist. They are spinning. That is arguably why these approaches exist at all. Each approach, however, is abstractly the same. They all try to tie two independent things together, and in the end, this fails logically and mathematically. It is for these reasons I argue changes in efficiency, effectiveness, and productivity have no direct cash flow affect. Efficiency, for instance, often involves reducing the rate of capacity consumption and in that context it will not affect how you spend money. Being inefficient, ineffective, and unproductive may create a situation where you may need to buy more capacity than necessary or sooner than necessary to meet demand, but changing any or all of the metrics will not affect $cost_C$. This notion is critically important to understand and is covered in Chapter 12. If improvement opportunities and their business cases are heavily weighted in total value or magnitude by $cost_{NC}$, your cash flow improvements will not be realized as expected.[1]

---

[1] Reginald Tomas Lee, "How we Overstate ROI on Improvement Projects," *Cost Management*, November/December 2015.

CHAPTER 16

Do You Need Accounting?

Accounting and accounting data have taken center stage with managerial decision-making for many decades. As a result, understanding and managing costs, and reporting desirable profit numbers has become the focus of many leaders and executives. The key question, though, is: Should it? Do you need accounting and accounting data to run your company? The answer is: No. Let me explain.

Let's consider accounting dynamics from two perspectives. One is from hindsight and the other is foresight.

Hindsight

When looking at accounting data in hindsight, you will see a scenario like one seen in Exhibit 16.1.

In this scenario, looking at it from the perspective of capacity and transaction dynamics, a couple of things should become clear. First, the reporting represents what happened through the analysis period. The one set of circumstances representing what was spent, what activities were performed, and the work output created happens between T_0 and T_F. All accounting can do post T_F, is describe what happened.

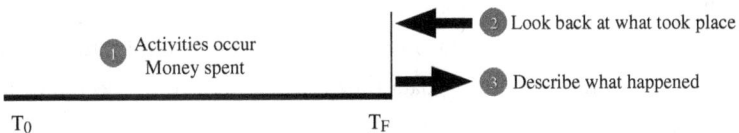

Exhibit 16.1 In hindsight, accounting describes what happened in the past. Spending on capacity and transactions has already taken place, and the work has been done. There is one, and only one, true description of the activities and cash transactions that took place between T_0 and T_F. Accounting then uses its assumptions and math to describe the true activities in its own way

As a result, when looking to a costing approach to improve your financials or reported data, the only thing that accounting can do in this case is represent the one set of circumstances in a way that is most desirable to you and your objectives. Its representation is limited by the circumstances that created it. For example, if you're looking for the lowest taxable income, you can describe what happened in a way that lowers your taxable income. If you want the highest profit, you can represent what happened another way that shows higher profits. However, what happened between T_0 and T_F will constrain the extent to which your situation can be described. Accounting can't, or at least shouldn't, suggest something happened that did not. What you do between T_0 and T_F determines, to a great extent, what your numbers are going to be. Hence, your accounting technique can only influence how the numbers are represented, but what you do, to a greater extent, determines what the accounting numbers can reflect. If you want lower $cost_{NC}$, reduce what you're buying that is allocable, then you'll improve both cash and the calculated profit.

This is an important point, so I will state it differently. If you want to improve your accounting numbers, accounting techniques will go only so far. If you want your performance to be improved to the highest desirable level, you have to focus on capacity and transactions, by getting in front of what is being analyzed—capacity and transactions—not focusing on the allocated data.

Data in Foresight

People and companies often do things to attempt to affect costs in foresight. They will make decisions that they feel will affect future costs positively and avoid decisions that may have negative cost implications. The reality is that the accounting data they use can negatively affect and, in fact, distort the picture of future cash flow.

One situation I often see involves overproduction or overbuying. These situations usually begin with focusing on the gross margin level or the unit cost level. The idea is that if you can reduce production costs or buy in bulk, the average cost for each unit goes down. This will encourage companies to overbuy or overproduce in the name of efficiency, lowering costs, and ultimately improving overall profit by improving gross margins. Two common examples of this follow. First, consider the company that overbuys. In the name of efficiency, they attempt to take advantage of a lower-pricing opportunity by buying more inventory than they need. What if a company needs only 40 items, but would be given a desirable unit price if they ordered 70, so they decide to buy more than they need? The situation is captured pictorially in Exhibit 16.2.

There's always the promise that the excess will be used. However, does anyone go back to validate this assumption?

In this case, paying a higher price leads to being more capacity productive even if, on the surface, it appears to be less cash efficient. In this case, buying the extra 30 leads to a $cost_C$ increase of about $270 (Exhibit 16.3). Along with this increased outflow is the risk of the 30 not being used. How many items do you have laying around your house, office, or warehouse that were bought due to a discounted selling price, only to have it go unused?

The second example involves overproduction. This, too, is a far too common example. The idea is simple. The assumption is that the more you do, the lower the average unit cost. Let's assume an order comes in

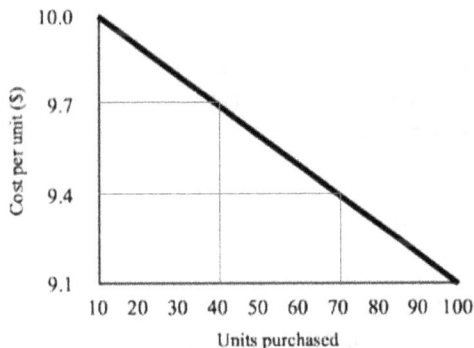

Exhibit 16.2 Assume there is demand only for 40 units. The desired price for the units is $9.40 per unit. The unit price is 30 cents per unit, more expensive at 40 units ($9.70) than it is at 70 units. This information might lead some to overbuy in the name of "saving money"

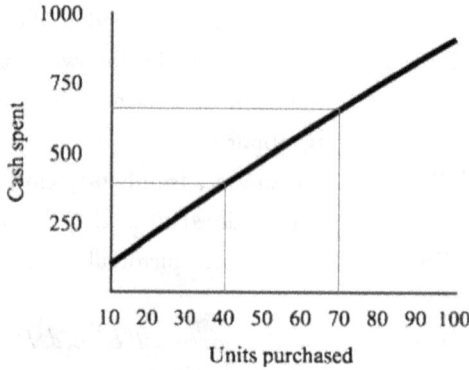

Exhibit 16.3 *When you focus on cash versus unit cost, you are led to the best cash flow decision. In this case, buying 30 more units when there was no demand for excess may not make much sense*

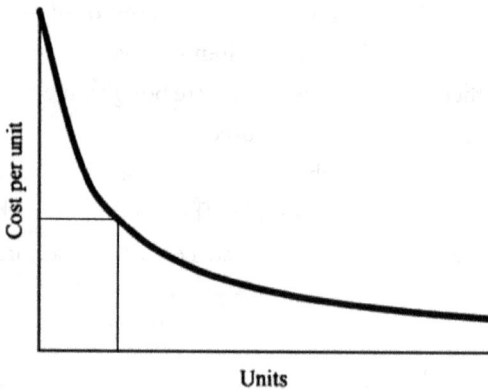

Exhibit 16.4 *Companies often look at certain output levels and determine their cost at that output level using this tool. The problem is, going back to Exhibit 15.8, what is this number telling you?*

for 500 coffee cups. You look at your cost curve and decide at 500 coffee cups, with a markup for profit added, the price would be too high. The anticipated selling price for each cup may, for instance, exceed the calculated cost for each cup (Exhibit 16.4).

You decide, therefore, to double your production to 1000 to get a lower unit cost and, therefore, fall into the desired price range once profit is added. In essence, you doubled your output to lower your cost$_{NC}$ so that you could make more money (Exhibit 16.5). Let's examine this decision further.

If you already had the capacity to produce 1,000 coffee cups, the marginal changes in $cost_C$ are nominal—basically, utilities involved in producing the 500 additional cups and possibly other incidentals. However, what if you didn't have the capacity? What if you had to buy the materials, buy more equipment, hire temporary labor to produce the additional 500 cups? Real cash, $cost_C$, is spent in the name of reducing a noncash number, $cost_{NC}$, and the spending actually will likely go unnoticed by accounting until someone paints a complete picture of the transaction.

Remember when I asked you if you would produce 20 of something if there were demand only for five? This is that scenario. Logically, you would make one decision, but somehow, in the midst of doing business and with alternate data presented, or pressure from management, we do illogical things.

Another example is Six Sigma and lean-type programs. As teams invade offices looking for efficiencies that lead to cost reductions, the focus is on reducing process cost, $cost_{NC}$. The financial justification often focuses and relies on allocated costs. Since $cost_{NC}$ is mostly capacity, the improvement opportunities often involve capacity efficiency—getting more with what you have, by creating more output or reducing the effort required to reach current levels of demand (Exhibit 16.6). This leads to the perception of big financial savings that will not likely be realized.

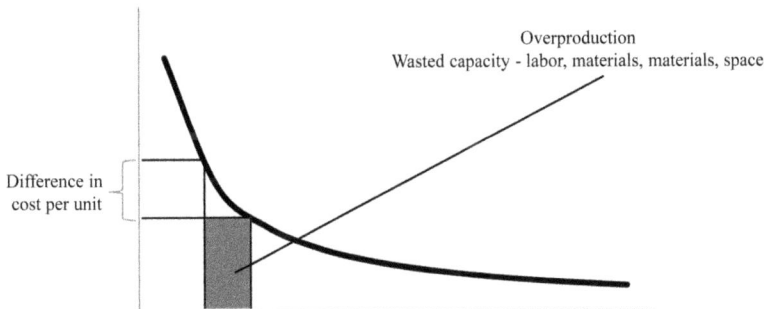

Exhibit 16.5 By focusing on the unit cost curve and average costing, companies often spend more money and waste their capacity to produce more and create a lower unit cost

The focus of the improvement is on this amount. There is a cost$_{NC}$ dollar amount that is applied to this savings. For instance, by saving time, we can reduce the cost of an invoice by $3. With the 30,000 invoices we process, we save $90,000. This is how leaders are bamboozled.

Exhibit 16.6 Many improvement approaches seek to calculate dollar savings. These dollar savings are often cost$_{NC}$, and because cost$_{NC}$ can often be large numbers due to the pervasiveness of wasted use of capacity, managers and leaders often get excited over the money they and their teams can save. They rarely see these numbers, because they are not real

The solutions often suggest lower costs, but the cost that is lower is cost$_{NC}$. Cost$_C$ has not changed. This was once represented in a debate I had with someone who is acknowledged to be well-versed in costing. He explained how implementing some sort of a handheld technology saved, let's say, $15 per transaction. He believed this to be true. It may have saved $15 in cost$_{NC}$, but it saved no direct dollars, cost$_C$. What it saved was time, and in this case, time was not money. It was just time.

Cost accounting paints a partial picture of operations and cash flow, and can distort the reality of how what you do affects what you make. Accounting approaches were created to report what happened, not to manage your business. Remember, cash is king. If, by using cost accounting approaches, you can destroy cash or promise cash improvements where they aren't, how is it a productive tool? To answer the question at the beginning of the chapter, the answer is: No. Other than for reporting purposes, you do not need accounting.

CHAPTER 17

Getting Managerial Information from Capacity

As mentioned previously, my guess is that you're probably thinking this; "I get what you're telling me, Reginald, but I still need my accounting data. If I don't have it, how will I replace it?" I'd like to propose that the answer is: Replace it with data from modeling and managing capacity.

Capacity modeling is somewhat of a unifying concept between finance, accounting, and operations. Let me explain. Finance and accounting seek to understand, explain and manage the financial state and performance of your company. In the context of understanding the financial state of your company, cash flow *should* be pretty easy to model. Most of what you buy and use to do work is capacity. How much and when you buy affects cash and the timing of cash flows. How efficiently you use it affects how much you need to buy. What you create to sell may affect how much money you receive. Since all this happens ahead of accounting processing the data to provide reporting information accounting can only describe all this in hindsight. It cannot model the future effectively, and management is often about planning for the future.

Having spent the last two decades doing cash flow modeling and modeling capacity, I personally feel it is a much more accurate and precise way of looking at, and understanding organizations in a way accounting can never offer, and it's easier for operations people to understand and manage. There are three reasons why I believe this is the case:

1. Capacity modeling is more precise, accurate, and simpler when modeling cash flow than accounting.
2. It provides necessary operational data and serves as the foundation of information that is used by both accounting and operations.

3. It can explain the accounting results simply, whereas accounting cannot explain capacity data without extreme effort

Modeling

As mentioned before, when I sought to understand the profit equation, I realized due to accounting rules and procedures, that profit doesn't represent making money, and cost$_{NC}$, a cost type used to calculate profit, does not represent spending money.

When I began modeling cash, the basic premise was, changes in cash must equal money received minus money spent. I had to model these factors effectively. This meant cash flow cost, cost$_C$, had to be accurate when modeling money leaving the company. When does money leave the company? When you pay for something. That's it. You could be buying capacity, paying for a transaction, or paying an obligation such as taxes and royalties, but in the end, that is when money leaves your company.

When you look at cash flow modeling from a capacity perspective, there is a level of clarity you gain. You know when money comes in and why. You know when money leaves and why. You can understand why you had changes in cash flow and to what extent you had them. Contrast this with cost accounting, where you can become more efficient and claim cost savings and even improvements in profit when no cash was saved![1] Consider, too, things like working capital, where inventory items, sitting on the balance sheet with one of many possible values determined using arbitrary allocation techniques are considered equally with cash, accounts payables, and accounts receivables. Does this make sense to you?

When I speak of capacity cash flow modeling, I compare it to having raw healthy ingredients. I have a tomato, onion, garlic, and perhaps basil. I see these ingredients and I know what I have, I know its value, and they're easy to understand. Cost accounting, however, creates store bought spaghetti sauce; some good things like tomatoes got mixed in with some bad things like preservatives, chemicals, and who knows what else, and

---

[1]This is described in some detail in At Issue: Are Cost Savings Mirages? (2014). Business Dynamics & Research. Retrieved from http://bdrco.org/BDR/Publications_files/Are%20Cost%20Savings%20Mirages.pdf

the result is a mixture of stuff we call spaghetti sauce. You may or may not know or understand it and how it was made. In the end, you just know you have spaghetti sauce. Similarly, when you mix raw capacity and cash data, good healthy numbers, with allocations, assignments, and arbitrarily created relationships, you end up with numbers that you may not know or understand where they came from. It's spaghetti sauce for your business.

Capacity data clarifies matters. Accounting numbers cause companies to do things like sell off products or service lines prematurely because of the perception or belief that it is not making enough money. And what proxy for making money is used? Profit, the concept I argued had nothing to do with making money. It's spaghetti sauce. This leads to companies selling off divisions that are making money only to have the executives realize that their relative capacity levels are higher after selling off the revenue source without having the revenue to offset it. This leads to poor decision-making in key areas such as outsourcing decisions.

Capacity, on the other hand, looks at the situation differently. The first question is: Is profit the right proxy to use when making this decision? Depending on the allocation approach used, product or service lines can be cash cows and consume little capacity, yet be over taxed on the cost side leading to the belief that it is not as profitable as it should be. The money-making criterion should be how much money the product or service generates given the resources it consumes; efficiency. Accounting does not directly tell you that. The second question to ask is; "If we lose this revenue source, we do not have this cash coming in. What are we going to stop buying to offset this revenue loss?" It's not about allocating costs differently or anything other than what are you buying now, and what are you going to stop buying after you no longer have that money coming in.

I regularly see companies giving groups and divisions the options to buy from external sources when these sources may be competing against internal sources. For example, a college chose to cost the production of copies so this value could be charged to its academic departments. Let's say this cost was seven cents a copy. So, departments, looking to save money, went outside to buy copies for $0.05 per copy. This transaction *increased* the college's cost$_C$. Why? Because the college bought and paid for the capacity to make copies. Most of this cost existed regardless of whether the department bought copies from it or not. But now, the department decided to also give money to external providers. The culprit? Cost$_{NC}$, the calculated accounting cost, and not considering the capacity implications of the scenario. This meant more money left the college, putting the college in a worse cash flow situation by increasing cost$_C$, than there would have been otherwise, all in the name of the departments trying to reduce what was, to the college, cost$_{NC}$. Someone thought this value meant actual money, so it was charged back to the departments as if it were. This is just one of the many cash flow destroying decisions I see on a regular basis. Capacity modeling focuses on where money is being spent—buying capacity, and raises options in this context.

Models Operations More Effectively

I often cringe when I talk to people and organizations about their operations cost data. When I see a company overly focused on the cost of this or the cost of that, I know at this point, there is likely a true lack of understanding of capacity and, therefore, important operating and financial parameters associated with their company. And remember, capacity is likely their largest cost$_C$ category. Consider this example. Let's say gas is $4 and you average 20 miles per gallon. In this situation, you're looking at a cost$_{NC}$ $.20 per mile. By now, you know this doesn't represent spending money, but those who haven't read this book may not yet understand the difference. Now consider asking some simple scenarios.

Let's say all of a sudden the cost per mile goes up to $0.25. What happened? Well, it is unclear. Gas mileage could've gone down to 16 miles per gallon. Cost of gas could have gone up to $5. It could be a combination of both. The real answer is not clear, and would require further investigation. Compare this to scenarios in your company. Let's say you run a variance. Something should cost $3.29 and it ends up costing you $3.42. What happened? What is the source of the variance? In some cases, it might take a significant amount of time to trace the sources and describe what happened. What if you are asked to do the equivalent of reducing the cost to $0.16 per mile? What are your options? Think about how much time, effort, and systems information are required to keep track of this cost and what caused it to change. And all for an artificially calculated value that isn't even money. You spend lots of money trying to understand and manage numbers that are not money.

Here's another. Your cost is $0.20 per mile. How much gas do you need to drive 15 miles? The question is really, "How much capacity do I need to go 15 miles?" Again, a fairly simple question that you shouldn't need to be an accountant to answer. The answer, again, is: It's not clear. You have too many unknowns to solve this. You don't know the price of gas and you don't know fuel efficiency. Now, if you know you are getting 15 miles per gallon, the answer is: I need one gallon. Simple. Clear.

These are examples of issues we may encounter daily. How do I handle changes in efficiency? How much capacity will I need to meet a particular order? When I work with executives, one thing I try to help them see is, operations people should be working with operational data. As an operations person focused on capacity, I will monitor information related to how much capacity I have and how efficiently and productively I'm using it. This is what I can understand and manage intuitively, and the nice aspect is, you have all the capacity cash flow dynamics wrapped up with this information, creating a source for mathematical integrity between operations and operational data and financial data.

It's like keeping track of how many miles I am able to get from each gallon, and how many gallons I have rather than a cost per mile. I immediately know when I buy more expensive gas or when my gas mileage drops off. I have a sports car that gets 30 miles per gallon on the freeway, but the way I drive it, it gets around 10 miles per gallon or less in the city. I immediately know and can predict the financial impact without even considering cost per mile. I need three times as much gas driving in the city than when on the freeway. If driving 30 miles and gas tank is empty, I know one gallon or $4 may get me there. If driving 30 miles in stop and go traffic, I know $12 will get me there.

If city driving affects cost per mile, so be it, but it isn't important information. I understand the operating parameters and data, and can manage them to get output and the financial numbers I want (I have $6 in my pocket, can I make it to an ATM?). I can change my driving habits or look for cheaper gas if I need to go farther on less money. Contrast this with someone telling you to lower your cost per mile by $0.05. It is a much more ambiguous and difficult task to manage. If you need that number for some reason such as reporting, fine. However, translating it into operating parameters such as, "you have $40, you currently are getting 15 miles per gallon and to get to your destination without having extra money, you need to average 17 miles per gallon" will help someone understand how to achieve the objective more clearly.

The same applies to managing capacity levels. If I know I need to go a certain distance, or get a certain level of output from my capacity, I will start considering options to help me achieve this objective. For example, if I know I need three-fourths of a gallon to get to my destination, I can ask myself, do I have it? If so, there is no cost to me to drive there. If I don't have it, I know I will need at least three-fourths of a gallon, so do I buy just three-fourths? Fill up? I can make a decision based on the price of the capacity. If it's expensive, buy enough to get me to the point when it is cheaper. I can also ask a very important question from a managerial perspective—Can I get there by being more frugal?

When you understand your situation in this way, decisions are simpler, and the effects of the decisions are easier to understand. And the concepts are based on what people understand—what I have and what I need it to do. It is how we think. I have 10 slices of bread, how many sandwiches can I make? Ideally I can make five. Even your kids can solve this problem. We don't naturally think cost per bread slice. At $5 per loaf, how many loaves do I need? If I need 7 sandwiches, how much do I need to spend on bread? We know its $10. If you calculate a cost per slice of $0.50, does this mean you could spend $7 to make the sandwiches? Not if partial loaves are not available.

In this context, I propose capacity modeling helps people understand their operations more effectively. Capacity focuses on what you buy and how you use it. You know that if you manage your capacity inefficiently, you may have to buy more, and both your $cost_{NC}$ and $cost_C$ can go up. Let me explain.

I have suggested many times that efficiency will not directly improve cash flow. Making you more efficient doesn't mean you are paid less. However, what if I need many of you? Let's say you have a customer service agent and you can handle five calls per hour. If seven calls come in, you need two people. Assuming the same efficiency, if 12 calls come in, I will need three people. You can see the pattern in Exhibit 17.1. More demand may make me buy more capacity. This increases $cost_C$. Now, let's increase your efficiency to seven calls per hour. This means we could delay bringing in more capacity as demand increases. The investment is delayed, which aids in cash flow management as seen in Exhibit 17.2.

Improvement is manifested as a delay in spending. This suggests that efficiency doesn't reduce costs, it enables you to increase them more slowly. In times of reduction, efficiency enables you make decisions to

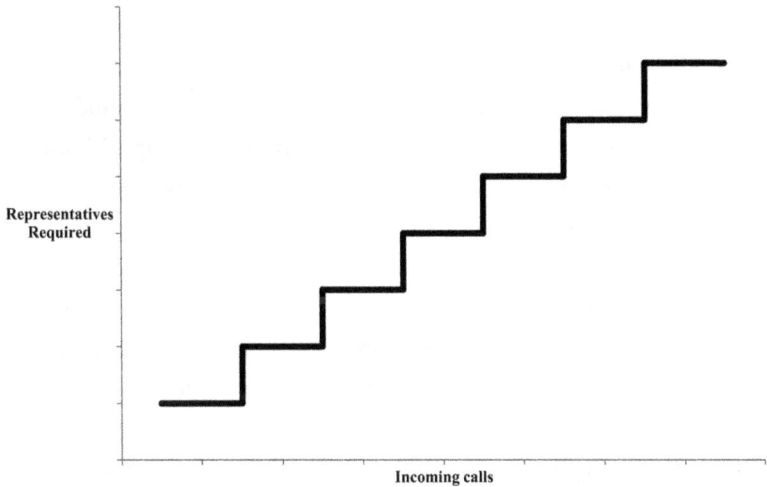

Exhibit 17.1 When your reps can handle five calls per hour, whenever incoming calls exceed a multiple of five, you have to add another rep. Hence, at 6, 11, 16, and so on, you would have to hire another rep

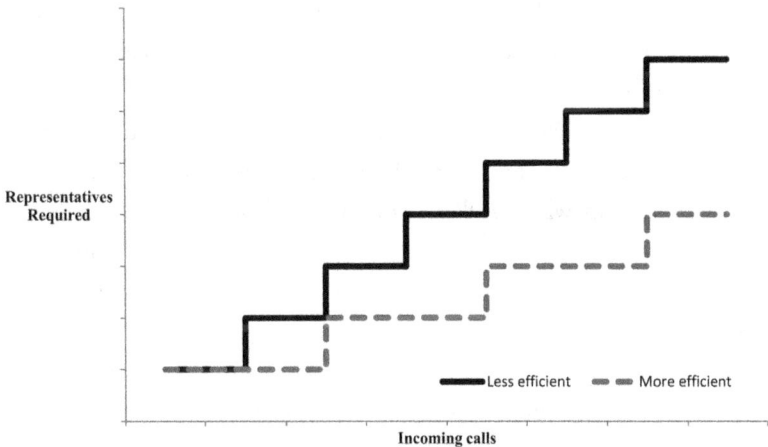

Exhibit 17.2 When you increase the capability to handle calls to seven, you can now delay hiring until you exceed multiples of seven. The result is that you can get more work done with less capacity, which enables your cost curve to increase more slowly

reduce costs faster. If demand were 20 calls at an output rate of five calls per person per hour, by increasing from five to seven, you can meet demand with three versus four people. As you reduce size, efficiency can enable you to buy less capacity to meet demand, thereby reducing $cost_C$. Notice, the term used is "enable" cost reduction. It does not "cause" cost reduction. You can still choose not to take advantage of opportunities that are available to you.

In the end, there's not an operating environment you can model with accounting data more effectively than you can by modeling with capacity. This is both from an operational and a financial perspective. Capacity is what you buy and use, so the financial information and the data you get from modeling capacity is accurate because it is the source of the data. Accounting, in contrast, creates relationships that do not exist and it can change the timing of when financial transactions occur. Which seems right to you? It's like trying to describe you when looking straight at you versus trying to describe you in one of those funhouse mirrors that distorts the perception of you. By modeling the capacity, you have the operating data you need, you have the $cost_C$ data you need, and you also have all the inputs that accounting should use for reporting purposes.

This is why I call capacity modeling the unifying idea of operations and finance. Dealing with the raw data of what you buy, what you have, and what you do with it is what operations focuses on. What you bought and the financial implications of what you created based on a set of rules set forth by a governing body is the focus of accounting. They all intersect with capacity. In the end, all information you need to manage and make better decisions starts with and is enabled by capacity.

The simplicity when working with capacity lends itself to both operations and accounting. From an operational perspective, I am working in units that operations understands. From a financial perspective, I can take this data and begin to describe what happened operationally using financial language. It becomes much easier to model the financial implications of how you operated in the past or choose to operate in the future, and to project the financial impact of changes you'd like to make to your operations. Additionally, consider what happens when accounting describes a past operating period. Depending on the technique you use, your costs can change. There is no unique description of what happened. Contrast this with capacity modeling, where there is only one description of what happened. Descriptions of capacity and capacity use are unambiguous, and this leads to greater clarity.

Serves as an Intersection between Operations and Accounting

When you model operations from a capacity perspective, money is inherently brought along for the ride. You cannot holistically consider input capacity without considering the $cost_C$ to have it. When you consider the transaction, you buy input, you enable the creation of output, and from there, you create work products.

When you consider this process objectively, the data and information are very clear. You know how much input you bought. You don't know exactly how much output you will get, of course, because there are a number of factors that affect output capacity. However, if you consider historical performance, you may gain some insights so you can predict the amount of output capacity generally involved with creating the work products from a planning and budgeting perspective. Once finished, the answers are clearer regarding how much output each work product consumed. The cycle, then, is to consider how much you bought, how you used it, and what you got from it.

A simple example is buying bread to make sandwiches. You spend $5 and you get 20 slices. You should be able to make 10 sandwiches. In the end, you make nine. From the situation, it is clear—you spent $5, got nine sandwiches, and there is either one or two pieces—that were not involved in sandwich production. We can go back and find out pretty easily what happened with the unused bread. They may have been heels, and since people may not like them in sandwiches, we adjust our expected output. One or both could have been damaged. Perhaps, there was demand only for nine, so the two are able to be used in other sandwiches.

Consider cost accounting information. The objective is to determine a cost. How much capacity you brought and the operating details are secondary to the drive toward calculating this non-cash cost if considered at all. So, you might do a number of things. You may use average costing to determine each slice of bread cost you $.25. So each sandwich costs $.50

in bread. In this case, I spent $4.50 on sandwiches and had $.50 in waste. Or, we can allocate this $5 into productive sandwich making and put the unused bread into a waste account or. . . .

The point here is that the capacity approach is clean. When people start creating accounting data, they begin to lose track of the true activities that happened in operations. You buy five dollars' worth of bread and you used 18 slices to make nine sandwiches. If you want to calculate cost$_{NC}$ of a sandwich, you are free to do so. In the end, what does it tell you that is useful operationally or financially?

These reasons cause me to believe that the best way to get your arms around operations and cash flow is to focus on managing capacity. If you focus on capacity, the raw data—the tomatoes, onions, garlic, and basil—you can begin to manage it much more clearly and effectively than when you turn the raw data into spaghetti sauce. The number of a-ha moments clients have had when explaining these ideas has been astounding. Many suggest the ideas were common sense in hindsight, but mind blowing in foresight. Many things make sense in hindsight; hence, the cliché "hindsight is 2020." However, what may be more important than seeing things in hindsight, is your ability to see them in foresight—20/20 foresight. Wouldn't it be nice to have 20/20 foresight? Capacity thinking gets you closer to 20/20 foresight than accounting ever will.

PART 3

CHAPTER 18

Explicit Cost Dynamics Revisited

About 15 or so years ago, I published my first book project. The title of the book is *Explicit Cost Dynamics: An alternative to activity-based costing*. This approach is the basis for the capacity and cash flow modeling suggested throughout this book. At first, the idea seemed to be catching on. I had a number of really cool clients and met some remarkable business people. After a while, the idea somewhat fizzled. In my opinion, there are a number of reasons why that happened.

1. The book and the idea were complicated.
2. I was not interested in pushing the concept.
3. My lack of maturity in developing the ideas.

Complicated

Explicit Cost Dynamics, or ECD, evolved from my PhD studies. I studied engineering and had a very strong math background. This combination can lead to questionable assumptions about how the world views things versus how an engineer might. For example, the math of ECD was built based on how an engineer or a mathematician would go about solving a problem using math. Once finished, I looked at it and thought, "Ah, yes. Simple. Elegant. Everyone will get it!" Wrong. I often think about folks on LinkedIn and Facebook who get the arithmetic problems wrong—you know the ones:

You're The Next Einstein If You Can Figure This Out:

$$1 + 1 + 1 + 0 + 1 \times 0$$

You get answers ranging from 0 to 2,156. In retrospect, some of the folks I've seen get these things wrong could have been people I would hope would understand ECD.

Another bad assumption or belief I had was, "Hey, if I just talk about the ideas, justify them with math, and publish it, people will pick it up and run with it." Again, wrong! There were three groups of people I found in the readership. There were the *advanced thinkers*, people who understood ECD and latched on to the idea immediately. There were leaders from this group who came to me and said, "I read your book and I want to implement this in my organization now." Working with these leaders was fantastic. I learned so much from them and their companies. The next group was the *tire kickers*. I am not sure this group ever truly grasped the idea. They would write or call to learn more, they asked lots of questions, but in the end, I'm not sure they did anything. Then there was a *hostile* group.

The hostile group dynamics were interesting to understand. The group was composed primarily of cost consultants and cost accountants with whom these ideas directly conflicted. This group was very quick to let me know their opinions or how they felt about my ideas, and they often were not rated PG-13! On one end of the spectrum, the nice end, there were passive aggressive folks. On the opposite end are people whom I hoped never got my address and found out where I lived.

The interesting thing about the hostile group is that they *never* fought the math. They could never argue why ECD was wrong mathematically. They would attack me for my knowledge of accounting, but they were never able to explain away the validity of the math. I'm not sure if this is because they thought it was right, that they did not take the time to truly understand it, or they tried and could not understand or disprove it.

When I look back at the book, I realized it had some really revolutionary ideas in it, but it isn't the easiest book to read. I remember being at a book signing at Disney World. There was an author ahead of me, a young African American male, who had written a book called *Chocolate Thoughts*. He did a reading from his book. He and the crowd were both really into it. He had a cool display with a huge picture of himself, lots of books, and he obviously knew what he was doing. I had only been to one book signing before. I did not know what I did not know. I did not have a huge display. I just threw few books in my suitcase and got on the plane.

So here I was following Mr. Chocolate Thoughts and all I could think about was leaving. Immediately! Instead, when it was my turn, I stood up and told a crowd, "After that I'm sure you don't want me to read you a bunch of math equations. That will not interest you. Instead, let me tell you about this concept, how it came about, and what its implications will be." To my surprise, they really enjoyed the presentation.

In the end, my writing and writing style did not make information as accessible as I would have liked. There was a lot of really good information in there and the foundation is very strong, although it has evolved tremendously since.

Did Not Push the Idea

To be honest, I did not write the book to become famous or to make millions of dollars. I was still thinking as an academic, so I wanted to put an intellectual stake in the ground. The book was that stake. Although I had the opportunity to work with great people and companies, I was not really interested and pushing the idea. People regularly asked about updates since the first book came out. Although there are dozens of articles and white papers based on ECD, there has not been a formal publication based purely on ECD since the book came out.

Immature Understanding

When I first wrote the book, I did not know a lot about accounting. I knew enough to be dangerous and to know it did not work from a cash flow perspective. However, I did not know enough about the intricacies of accounting. Also, believe it or not, I did not know a lot about my concepts either. Imagine that! I understood the math deeply, but I did not know as much as I would have liked regarding how to apply it and teach others how to use it in their organizations. That mature knowledge and understanding was lacking, so I was limited in my ability to help others use it.

I still believe in the power of Explicit Cost Dynamics, and use the concepts today to model cash dynamics and capacity dynamics with clients. Since it came on the scene, there have been many updates to the concepts and language, but I believe it is the most solid approach to understanding operations and cash flow out there. So, you may be wondering, what is this Explicit Cost Dynamics idea?

CHAPTER 19

What is Explicit Cost Dynamics?

Explicit Cost Dynamics is what resulted from the cash flow modeling I mentioned earlier in the book that was created to address challenges that were created by accounting. At the time, I had not understood the differences between $cost_C$ and $cost_{NC}$. I thought all costs should be defined as what I now call $cost_C$ and that would ensure they were aligned with cash flow. This was an area of major contention with many in the accounting field. They defined costs differently, and so when we would talk about costs, although we used the same word, what we were talking about was vastly different.

The idea behind ECD is fairly simple. At its most basic level, ECD looks at what your cash obligations are and provides information about what is required to become cash-wise profitable—to have a positive $profit_C$. It is entirely based on math and cash.

The approach starts with modeling cash obligations. If you stop all activities in your company, everything, what would you be paying for? In most cases, you'd be paying for input capacity. Again, that's your people, space, materials, information technology, and equipment. Next, what other $cost_C$ would you incur as you start to transact business? This could be anything from costs to take care of facilities, maintenance, and service contracts, to the $cost_C$ from selling new opportunities or any other types of cash-based transactions associated with operating the company. All of these costs will exist as a part of normal operations. However, clearly documenting and understanding input capacity is a huge component of getting the model right when it comes to modeling cash outflows.

This becomes your $cost_C$ basis. You need to make sure you're selling enough to offset these costs so that $profit_C$ is positive. This is different from accounting profit or $profit_{NC}$.

To have a positive profit$_C$, you have to generate more cash revenue during the period than you spent in the same period. Most of this revenue will come from selling products and or services. Sometimes, companies will incur costs, cost$_C$, to provide the products and services. For example, assume to provide the services you offer, you have to contract work with a third party to help you execute the services. This may be a cash transaction incurred specifically due to and because of delivering your services. Your selling price must be greater than the cost$_C$ incurred in executing or implementing your product or service. Note, if your people are involved in delivering the solution, it is cost$_{NC}$, and is not considered in this calculation, only the calculation of the cost obligations.

This leads to the idea that there are two levels of profit$_C$ that must be considered. Overall, the company should focus on having a positive profit$_C$, consider it a macro profit$_C$. Second, there is a profit$_C$ associated with providing your products and services, a micro profit$_C$. The micro profit$_C$ you make from selling your products and services contributes to paying off the capacity and transaction costs you incur while running your company so that you can have a positive macro profit$_C$. One client called this *giving back to the kitty*, suggesting that all projects have to give back enough to make the company cash-wise profitable. On the surface, one would propose that accounting can do the same thing. This is not true. Let me explain.

In the first part of the book I talked about why accounting profit was very different from cash flow. There were three primary reasons. First, accounting does an extremely poor job modeling cash. Second, capacity and transaction costs are not made salient by cost accounting, so there is no focus on them. We have discussed these two. Third, the idea of contributing cash sounds a lot like contribution margins. They are not really close to one another. Let's discuss this one further.

Contribution Margins and Fixed Versus Variable Costs

I noticed a number of clients and prospects who have used the idea of a contribution margins. Contribution margins seek to understand the cash contribution of an order. The basic premise is: When you create a product, perform a service, or fulfill an order there is interest in knowing the cash contribution of that order. People recognize the idea that there are costs that have nothing to do with the order, costs such as overhead. These costs are considered fixed. Instead of looking at the margin on the product, service or order by subtracting the "total" cost, why not subtract just the variable component? If you subtract the variable costs from the revenue, you should have the cash contribution. The most common costs that vary from an accounting perspective are materials and labor.

Although the logic makes sense, the approach does not work for two reasons:

1. Variable costs do not vary from a cash perspective.
2. Cost of goods sold is too limited in scope.

Fixed and Variable Costs

Accounting has this idea of fixed and variable costs. A fixed cost does not change with output. Variable costs do change with output. So, assume you're calculating the cost of a single item. Costs that may be applied to that product, such as supervision costs, may not change as you increase output. However, increased output increases labor and material costs, again, from an accounting perspective.

Accounting has this all wrong from a cash perspective. When you buy someone's time and the materials they will use to make things that you sell, the cash is in the transaction of acquiring them. Their $cost_C$ is independent of how you use them, yet accounting seeks to assign that cost to the output anyway. Recall, costing a local phone call. If each piece of output consumes labor and materials, these costs are seen as changing, hence variable (Exhibit 19.1). This value is $cost_{NC}$. Mathematically, cumulative $cost_{NC}$ *should* increase as you consume more capacity. However, $cost_C$ stays the same.

When accounting discusses fixed and variable costs changing, they may be $cost_C$ or $cost_{NC}$. An example of $cost_C$ that changes may be utilities, where you may use more to create more. However, with most contribution margin calculations include values that are $cost_{NC}$ and do not vary

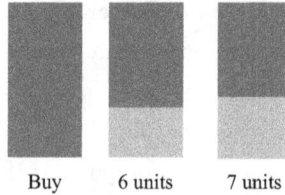

Buy   6 units   7 units

Exhibit 19.1 Doing work will consume input capacity. Since accounting seeks to put a cost on consuming input, the more input you consume, the greater the total cost. Notice cost$_C$ doesn't change, although the accounting cost increases

from a cash perspective. Since they do not vary from a cash perspective, the answer the contribution margin gives you will not reflect your cash dynamics.

Cost$_C$ varies only with how much you buy, the price you pay, or both. That is it. If you want to focus on how, what, and why cash costs vary, look at what you are buying and how you pay for it and not at accounting's definition of what is fixed and variable.

Scope of Analysis

Many contribution margin (CM) analyses focus on the gross margin (Equation 19.1):

$$CM = Revenue - Variable\ component\ of\ COGS \qquad (19.1)$$

The problem is, there may be costs outside the gross margin analysis that may change with a new order. For example, what if you have to pay transportation costs, taxes, or you take foreign exchange hits to cash with each order? These are often not considered in contribution margin discussions, but may be cash values that exist or are created due to fulfilling an order. Additionally, contribution margin analyses will not predict the need for additional capacity. Assume, to meet an order, you need to buy new equipment. There may be a cash transaction involved with fulfilling this order that will not show up in a gross margin analysis.

When you consider these factors, clearly accounting and contribution margins are ineffective at understanding and modeling cash transactions.

If we want to manage and improve cash flow management, we must focus on cash flow, not accounting metrics.

Focusing on Cash Using Capacity

The objective, ultimately, is to make more cash than you spend. The way to know whether you are doing this is to focus on, and manage cash inputs and outputs. To get your arms around what you are spending, focus on cash transactions, especially capacity. When considering cash requirements from revenues, you must be aware of how much cash you need to cover your obligations and the rate you are bringing it in.

Most cash inputs come from sales transactions. There should be targets for how much cash your organization should bring in on a periodic basis to offset its cash outputs. It is amazing how many companies do not know this simple information. It is mostly because people tend to focus on accounting data instead, and assume that if the accounting data suggests you're profitable, then you are cash flow positive. We know this is not true, and here is a very dangerous example; pricing based on margins.

Many companies will price based on adding a margin to their costs. First, what cost are they going to use? Remember, there are several ways to calculate a cost. Second, although the concept seems right, let's create a simple scenario. Let's say a company creates pencils and it calculates the cost to be $2. The company decides it will mark up the pencils to $2.50 so that it *makes* $0.50 off each pencil. Let's say the company sells 100,000 pencils. It should have made $50,000. What if the operating costs were $60,000? From an accounting perspective, you have not made enough money even if every transaction was profitable. With ECD, the focus is on understanding what your operating costs are and what you need to generate to cover them. If you have $60,000 in operating costs, you will need to sell enough pencils at such a micro net profit$_C$ so that the cumulative profit$_C$ covers the $60,000 at a minimum. If you adjust the price so that the net profit$_C$ on each pencil is $1, you will need to sell 60,000 of them. If the net profit$_C$ is $5, you will need to sell 12,000 of them. This approach, as with capacity, provides clearer guidance and clarity when used. It is tomatoes and garlic. Cost plus with allocated costs is spaghetti sauce.

If you know how much revenue you have coming in and how much you have going out, and if you model and manage this effectively, you will be in a position to assess your cash flow position accurately and make decisions that can improve it. Operationally and from the perspectives of the market and growth, you will want to grow the difference between revenues and cost$_C$, but you know that if you're bringing in more money than you spend, you will generally be okay.

This is what ECD is about. With input capacity at its core, it provides information about how much cash you are spending, where it is going, and helps you understand your overall cash position. It is the tool that is used to model cash flow and provide simple and powerful information back to leaders without overwhelming them with irrelevant data and information. Along with capacity dynamics, ECD creates a comprehensive and powerful way to see, understand, and manage all activities throughout an organization.

One of the weaknesses of the approach as it was developed is that given its focus on cost$_C$, it failed to acknowledge and offer an alternative to cost$_{NC}$. As a result, the model was quite rigid and did not offer a way for those who felt they needed this number to get the information they wanted. Subsequently, I have added the concept of *worth* to fill this gap.

CHAPTER 20

Worth

By now you will hopefully come to the conclusion that cost$_{NC}$ is of little value and does little more than create confusion. You do not really need it unless someone from the outside requests it. For example, if a customer asks you for your costs as a part of your relationship with them, you will have to calculate and provide them. In these cases, I've proposed that instead of using the idea of a cost, we use the idea of worth.

Understanding Worth

Let's say you bought 10 pounds of flour for $10. We know that the cost transaction was buying the flour. Using a pound will not cost you $1. It will not cost you anything. It is consuming capacity you have already purchased. In that context, all you really need is to determine a reasonable value for consuming that flour. This is where worth comes in.

When we use a pound of flour, we may say we have used *a pound's worth of flour*. Worth represents an amount or value of how much flour was used. The amount consumed is in capacity units, or CU. CU represents how you buy capacity. For instance, you buy labor, generally, in time. You buy space in square units such as square feet. You bought 10 pounds and consumed one of the 10 pounds. You have nine pounds left. If you need a dollar value for the capacity consumed, I generally recommend dividing the price you bought the capacity for by the amount of CUs you bought. For example, in this case you have purchased 10 pounds (pounds is the CU) of flour for $10. Each pound is worth $1. Notice this is not a cost. Using one pound does not cost you anything. It is an attempt to put a value on each of the 10 pounds of flour that you bought. It takes away the value of one pound versus another by considering them all equal. You can do this with any capacity you buy and use any relevant CU. If you pay someone $400 to work an eight-hour day, each hour is worth $50. A meeting that lasts two hours uses two hours' worth of capacity or $100 worth of capacity.

I chose the term worth for two reasons. First, by using the term cost, people will believe it is, and behaves like cash. It does not. Worth eliminates that confusion. A meeting uses $1,000 worth of capacity tells you something about the consumption of what you paid for. Saying a meeting costs $1,000 conjures up images of money leaving your company, which it does not. Additionally, it can reflect relative value. If four senior members of the company are in a one hour meeting, we might expect it might be worth more from a time perspective than a meeting with four co-op students.

The second reason is that worth aligns with capacity really well. First, speaking specifically about capacity, you will know how much capacity you have and how much you've used because you are still working in CUs. For example, you fill your gas tank up, go on a trip to a friend's house, and you come back home. You have a half tank of gas left. You know the trip took *a half tank's worth* of gas. You know, then, that you have a half tank left. If you know your tank size, 20 gallons for instance, you can say you've used about 10 gallons worth of gas. Figuring out what you have and what you have used becomes much more clear when considering the CUs that you buy.

The second thing this allows you to do is tie what you paid to how you consumed it. If you bought gas at $4 per gallon, you can say each gallon is worth $4, and your trip consumed $40 worth of gas. It did not cost you $40, that is the value of what you consumed.

I recommend to people that they use worth to keep track of $cost_{NC}$ information. If you absolutely have to have dollar value for capacity consumed, instead of reporting a cost, consider reporting worth and call it a cost if you must.

You may ask, "Without costs, how can I determine whether my products are profitable or not?" The simple answer is, you will not know if you have costs! There is not one true profit. First, remember, there are any number of costs that can be calculated for your product, and each one involves creating arbitrary relationships. Since there is not one cost, there is not one profit. If there is not one profit, how do you know which one is right? And again, we are not dealing with cash-based costs so what is profit telling you? So how valuable is the number? If you really needed a number, compare the capacity consumed to the revenue generated. This is a representation of efficiency and can be used to compare the efficient delivery of products and services.

Second, there is a bigger issue considering the profit of products, customers, and the notion of make versus buy analyses. Those devoted to accounting will assume these types of analyses are fine. You can consider the revenue two products bring in, subtract out the costs associated with them, and determine which is more profitable. You could look at customers, how much revenue they generate versus the cost to serve them, and determine customer profitability. Finally, there is the idea of whether we should make something or outsource it to another company or even another country.

With each of these analyses, you are ultimately subtracting costs from revenues. Assume for the moment we are considering cash revenues only. Some of the costs being subtracted from cash revenues are $cost_C$ numbers, which are cash. However, many, if not most, of the costs and customer and product line profitability calculations are not cash. For instance, activity-based costing analyses consider how much time and effort one customer consumes versus another and calculates a cost for this. This cost is $cost_{NC}$. Folks will take this noncash number and subtract it from a cash number to calculate what is, to them, an important cash-based financial value. Subtracting a noncash number from a cash number is like subtracting rocks from trees. This does not make sense.

What is worse is that this number has assumed meaning. I've seen many cases where if $cost_{NC}$ is greater than revenues, the product or service would be deemed unprofitable and actions would be taken. Does it make sense to subtract five rocks from three trees and assume, because the value appears to be negative it is bad? No, but the decision makers decide they will no longer offer the unprofitable product or service, or support what appears to be an unprofitable customer. There is a simpler way using the tools you have learned in this book:

1. Explicit cost dynamics
2. Worth
3. Efficiency

Explicit Cost Dynamics

Explicit cost dynamics will create understanding of where cash is coming from and going, and when. The focus will be on capacity and transaction costs and the rate of generating cash.

Worth

Worth becomes the basis for understanding more of the details behind capacity use and assigning a value to consumed capacity.

Efficiency

Finally, armed with this information, you can consider efficiency or productivity values to compare performance across products, services, or customers. The basis for the efficiency becomes how much revenue is generated compared to capacity used. Here's a simple example of how I use these tools for clients.

Let's say your kids want to create a sandwich shop for your neighbors. You tell them they must make money off of the setup. You buy a loaf of bread, with 20 slices for $5, two packs of cheese, 10 slices each, for a total of $8, and 25 slices of turkey for $10.

Explicit Cost Dynamics

You spent $23. Assume you charge them $5 to use the front yard. To breakeven on a macro scale, the kids will have to sell at least $28 in sandwiches. From what you bought, they should be able to make 10 sandwiches that have two slices of bread. Table 20.1 shows what the average price of a sandwich would need to be to break even.

Any issues in terms of using their materials inefficiently or having quality errors that would cause the number of potential sandwiches they could make given their starting capacity to go down would mean the average revenues from each sandwich would have to increase.

Worth

The first question is: What will the kids offer to sell. They decide to sell various types of sandwiches, as shown in Table 20.2.

Next, we look at the worth of the ingredients so we can calculate the value of the ingredients that goes into each sandwich (Table 20.3).

Table 20.1 The purpose of this analysis is to help you understand how much revenue you need to generate and how that ties to output capacity. It also helps you understand the importance of demand and quality. If you have quality issues and limit your output given the capacity you have, you have to make up that revenue with fewer sales opportunities. Second, and similarly, demand is critical. If there is little demand, as with quality, you have to make up your revenue with fewer sandwiches. It isn't about the unit margin, it is about the cash you have to earn.

Number of sandwiches	Average price
10	$2.80
9	$3.11
8	$3.5
7	$4.00
6	$4.67
5	$5.60
4	$7.00
3	$9.33
2	$14
1	$28

Table 20.2 The offering considers the use of the capacity involved to make it. This becomes the basis for worth calculations.

Offering	Description Two slices of bread included with each sandwich
Turkey	Bread with one slice of turkey
Turkey w/Cheese	One slice of turkey, one slice of cheese
Turkey w/Double Cheese	One slice of turkey, two slices of cheese
Double Turkey	Two slices of turkey
Double Turkey w/Cheese	Two slices of turkey, one slice of cheese
Double Turkey w/Double Cheese	Two slices of turkey, two slices of cheese

With this information, the kids can now begin to assign worth to each sandwich type. Of course, labor is left out here purely for the sake of simplicity, but it, and the other input capacity types, would be

Table 20.3 *The suggestion with work is that when you buy capacity, all capacity units (CUs) are worth the same from a consumption perspective. It doesn't mean some CUs will not generate more revenue. For instance, if you were to sublease office space you have, each square foot would be the same from a worth perspective, but space by windows or with a view may demand more revenue.*

Ingredient	Spent	Slices	Worth
Bread	$5	20	$0.25
Turkey	$10	25	$0.4
Cheese	$8	20	$0.4

Table 20.4 *The values here represent the value of all the ingredients used to create the sandwich. It is unbiased and simple to calculate.*

Offering	Worth
Turkey	$0.90
Turkey w/Cheese	$1.30
Turkey w/Double Cheese	$1.70
Double Turkey	$1.30
Double Turkey w/Cheese	$1.70
Double Turkey w/Double Cheese	$2.10

included where relevant in more comprehensive analyses. We can now look at the worth of the capacity consumed by each sandwich, found in Table 20.4.

The kids can now begin thinking about how much money they need to generate and what price they believe the market will support. They set the lowest price at $3.00, assuming, based on Table 20.5, if they only sell the minimum sandwich, they can break even if the demand is there. They set the other prices considering their perception of the relative value that the sandwich has in the market.

When you now compare the price to worth, there are two things that become immediately apparent. First, if you try to take the difference between price and worth, you will realize the number doesn't make sense mathematically. You cannot subtract numbers with dissimilar units. Recall subtracting rocks from trees. Second, the difference

Table 20.5 *These are the initially proposed prices. Proper pricing practices align price with the perception of value on the market. Note that although the Turkey is the lowest priced offering, if they sold 10 plain turkey sandwiches, they would still pay their cash obligations, but would not earn much of a salary!*

Offering	Price
Turkey	$3.00
Turkey w/Cheese	$3.50
Turkey w/Double Cheese	$3.70
Double Turkey	$4.50
Double Turkey w/Cheese	$5.00
Double Turkey w/Double Cheese	$5.50

Table 20.6 *This is the key information about each offering; the price and the worth. The tendency is to compare these two and calculate a profit. Do not do this. The worth does not take into account all that you bought and therefore spent cash on. Additionally, the numbers are dissimilar. One is a cash based value and the other is a calculated non-cash number. It only focuses on what you used. Therefore, there may be residual capacity you paid for that is not considered.*

Offering	Price	Worth
Turkey	$3.00	$0.90
Turkey w/Cheese	$3.50	$1.30
Turkey w/Double Cheese	$3.70	$1.70
Double Turkey	$4.50	$1.30
Double Turkey w/Cheese	$5.00	$1.70
Double Turkey w/Double Cheese	$5.50	$2.10

between the price of a turkey sandwich and the worth of the ingredients consumed is $2.10 (Table 20.6). If you multiply this $2.10 by the total possible sandwiches, 10, you get $21.00, suggesting there would be a $21.00 gross profit.[1] This does not happen. If you look at the money spent, you would gain $30 and you spent $23 on materials for a gross profit$_C$ of $7.00.

---

[1] Gross profit = revenues from sandwiches – cost of producing sandwiches, assumed to be the material costs in this case.

Efficiency

With price information and worth information, we can now look at efficiency. Efficiency in this context will help the kids consider how much revenue they are generating given the worth of their capacity consumed. This is a critical metric. Mathematically, you cannot calculate a cash-based profit for each sandwich because there is no $cost_C$ associated with creating a sandwich. However, you can take a look at which products consume the most resources and compare that to how much revenue you generate. Consider the Turkey w/Cheese and the Double Turkey (Table 20.7). Both consume the same value of capacity from a worth perspective, but the Double Turkey generates a full $1 more in revenue, suggesting it is a more efficient product. The same occurs with the Double Turkey w/Cheese versus the Turkey with Double Cheese. When you consider the efficiency of all products, the Double Turkey is the most efficient. Notice, if you tried to create a "profit" by subtracting worth from price, you will find the most efficient sandwich is not the most "profitable" one. Both the Double Turkey w/Cheese and the Double Turkey w/Double Cheese have a greater "unit profit."

You can also pick target efficiency levels and determine pricing. In Table 20.8, you can see the updated prices given the desire for all products to reach an arbitrarily chosen 3.46 efficiency level.

Table 20.7 With worth being the input and price being the output, you can calculate efficiency using the efficiency equation. Interpreting the date would be, "for every dollar of worth consumed, this sandwich generated this amount of revenue."

Offering	Price	Worth	Efficiency
Turkey	$3.00	$0.90	3.33
Turkey w/Cheese	$3.50	$1.30	2.69
Turkey w/Double Cheese	$3.70	$1.70	2.18
Double Turkey	$4.50	$1.30	3.46
Double Turkey w/Cheese	$5.00	$1.70	2.94
Double Turkey w/Double Cheese	$5.50	$2.10	2.62

Table 20.8 By targeting a certain efficiency value, you can determine the price. You can then compare the price to whether it can be sustained in the market.

Offering	Efficiency	Worth	Price
Turkey	3.46	$0.90	$3.11
Turkey w/Cheese	3.46	$1.30	$4.50
Turkey w/Double Cheese	3.46	$1.70	$5.88
Double Turkey	3.46	$1.30	$4.50
Double Turkey w/Cheese	3.46	$1.70	$5.88
Double Turkey w/Double Cheese	3.46	$2.10	$7.27

When using this approach, you have a significantly more information. You know how much revenue you need to generate, how much cash you have flowing out. You know how much capacity you have and which products, or customers, consume that capacity, and you can compare it to revenues generated. You can even compare products, product lines, or customers. I call this approach worth and capacity analysis, or WACA, and it has been a very valuable tool to help me understand the situations clients are in, and make recommendations that directly improve cash flow.

CHAPTER 21

The Red Pill

For those who took the blue pill, life will continue on blissfully, but they live with a significant level of risk. They'll believe that activities, products, and services cost money. They will overcalculate benefit opportunities. They will invest in projects with a questionable cash flow ROI. They will quote the cost of an invoice or the cost to handle a customer service call. They will continue to make decisions that they feel are best for their organization even though the logical and mathematical evidence suggests they're wrong.

For those who took the red pill, the business world will seem very different. There are three major areas where you will be able to outperform those who took the blue pill substantially. This is because you have a perspective on things that *they don't even know exists*. These examples are as follows:

1. Understanding the dynamics and limitations of profit
2. Understanding the dynamics of cost reduction
3. Improving the return on investment and reducing the risk of investments

Dynamics of Profit

When you think about the cash dynamics of profit, two things become apparent. The first focuses on the current period. The revenue you make now must offset your current $cost_C$ including the supporting infrastructure that enables further research and development for new products and services. It must also help support investments that will enable future growth. You will know if there are shortfalls and what you need to do about them.

Consider the pharmaceuticals industry. One big issue focuses on the cost to develop a new drug. There is relatively small $cost_C$ involved in performing research and development for a new drug. While there may be transactional costs associated with creating the drugs, a good percent of the $cost_C$ is tied up in the capacity infrastructure built up to support the research. You have expensive facilities and scientists. But ask yourself, if this same infrastructure existed, but for some reason, there were no drugs created, would the $cost_C$ of the capacity change? No. You have research and development capacity consuming cash doing their jobs. The quantification of this consumption is $cost_{NC}$. The output may be a new drug, or it may be a failure. Ultimately, the key is to create drugs for the future that will create enough revenue to pay for future $cost_C$. Today's drugs pay today's $cost_C$. The key is to be efficient and make drugs that will sustain future cash requirements and growth.

This is a controversial point of view, but it is what the cash flow and math says. You spend money now to pay current expenses and on things that will generate revenues both now and in the future.

For companies dealing with pricing products and services, the focus is not on what something costs to make. This number is not real. Instead, you focus on pricing based on market value and sell to generate revenues to offset cash flow costs at a minimum. When you need a financial value to use as a cost, you use worth to represent capacity consumption, but you understand that it is not a cost. It is just a way to represent capacity consumption.

Second you're not constrained by accounting. The focus is on the factors that affect $cost_C$, transactions and capacity, and you manage these. You know that when you manage capacity costs, you manage what gets allocated, which means you are affecting calculated $cost_{NC}$ as well. You know how much money is coming into your company and leaving it, regardless of what the accounting statements tell you.

Cost Reduction

When it comes to cost management, having taken the red pill, you understand the only way to reduce real costs, $cost_C$, is to buy less or buy cheaper. You understand that efficiency only improves capacity use, and to gain a cash flow improvement, you have to put yourself in a position to buy less or cheaper capacity. $Cost_{NC}$ does not really matter to you except when reporting for government or client purposes. You'll not be bamboozled by consultants looking for you to spend big bucks on cash savings you know will not materialize. And you know how to align improvement opportunities directly with cash flow and how to quantify the improvement. Your cost management techniques are far superior to those who have taken the blue pill.

Improved Investment

Many companies negatively affect the returns of their improvement investments and increase risk in three ways. First, they quantify the benefit opportunity incorrectly. Second, they do not project the savings correctly. Third, they do not go back to measure performance to plan.

Having taken the red pill, it is very clear what needs to be done to quantify benefits. When will you buy more or less capacity? How much will you buy? When will you get rid of excess capacity? How much money will you avoid spending as a result? You also understand the importance of transactions and the role they play when managing cash flow.

Tie this to your projected timing for the changes in capacity; you now have a projected cash flow timeline with clear requirements regarding what is necessary to achieve these numbers. Finally, you can close the gap between what you projected and what you realize. Your savings and improvements are tied to discrete decisions to add or subtract capacity and to what extent. You compare the assumptions to reality to make the necessary adjustments. You can approve projects based on the cash benefit of the project. This is not to suggest all projects are cash based, of course, but when cash is an issue and improved cash flow management is the objective, your analysis approach is very clear and weeds our poorly documented cost benefit analyses.

In the end, what I've offered is a simple way to look at your organization. Accounting math does not work. The output is unhealthy. It creates tomato sauce. You cannot go wrong when you are dealing with what is natural, whole, and simple. You cannot go wrong with the truth.

APPENDIX A

As mentioned in Chapter 7, efficiency is the math inverse or opposite of the average cost. It is important to understand this relationship because its implications are substantial!

Let's say you pay a customer service representative $15 to handle calls. The average cost per call curve can be seen in Exhibit A.1. From this curve we start to draw inferences. For example, as she handles more calls, the calculated cost per call goes down. Note, this is $cost_{NC}$ because you paid her $15 and that does not change with the number of calls she handles. It creates other curious scenarios as well. For instance, why don't costs decrease at the same rate throughout the curve? The cost drops significantly between the first and second calls, but not so much between the ninth and 10th calls. What is so special about the second call that its drop is so much more substantial than the 10th?

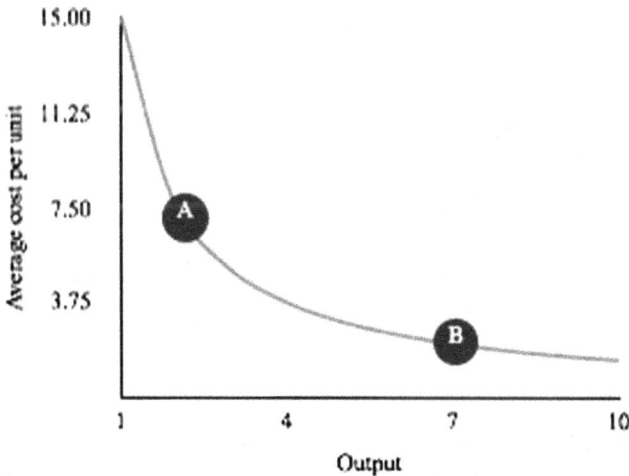

Exhibit A.1 *The average cost curve suggests more output at the same input costs reduces the average cost of the output. Hence, going from A to B supposedly leads to a lower cost. The average cost/unit for two units is more than twice that of seven, even though the cash requirement is the same whether there are two or seven units. It is easy to see why people err on the side of doing more*

Next, let's consider different salaries. If someone makes $10 per hour, their cost curve added to the one at $15 per hour creates the curves found in Exhibit A.2. Notice the curves represent one cost, either $10 or $15. Since each curve is the same cost, these are isocost or *same*-cost curves.

There are two key implications here. First, doing more for the same cost has no effect on $cost_C$ in this and similar cases. The cash is either $10 per hour or $15 per hour. Second, if you want to make a cash-based change, you have to move to entirely different curve. Moving down the same curve only affects $cost_{NC}$, not $cost_C$. Only when you make the jump to a different curve will $cost_C$ be affected.

This is an argument against the cost benefits of economies of scale. Doing more with the same inputs is believed to lower cost. It does lower $cost_{NC}$. All things being the same, and without additional action, $cost_C$, the most critical cost, doesn't go down with economies of scale. Why?

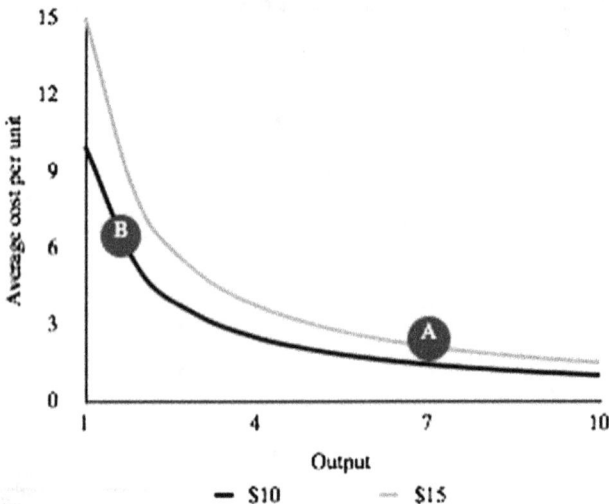

Exhibit A.2 *These are the isocost curves for $15 and $10. Assume your output is something like coffee mugs or sales calls. This chart suggests it is cheaper to make seven coffee mugs spending $15 than it is to make two mugs spending less. The same goes for sales calls. However, it is not cheaper to do more. There may be benefit if you sell more with increased output, but that is revenue, not cost. It is easy to see how companies can be enticed by the notion of doing more to "reduce" their costs*

The average cost per unit is determined by taking the cost of the hour $15 and dividing it by what it does, handle calls. Mathematically, this is

$$\text{Average cost per unit} = \$15/\text{Number of calls} \qquad (A.1)$$

Abstractly, this is what you start with, $15, which is input. It's a start. You then divide it by the output you created, calls. So the formula for the average cost per unit is

$$\text{Average cost per unit} = \text{Input} / \text{Output} \qquad (A.2)$$

Efficiency, on the other hand, is defined as output divided by input, as seen in Equation A.3. This suggests efficiency is just the math inverse or opposite of the average cost per unit. When you begin plotting efficiency of $10 and $15 dollars per hour, you will get the curve found in Exhibit A.3:

$$\text{Efficiency} = \text{Output} / \text{Input} \qquad (A.3)$$

The curve in Exhibit A.3 suggests that by getting more output at the same cost$_C$, you're just becoming more efficient. Cost$_C$ has not gone

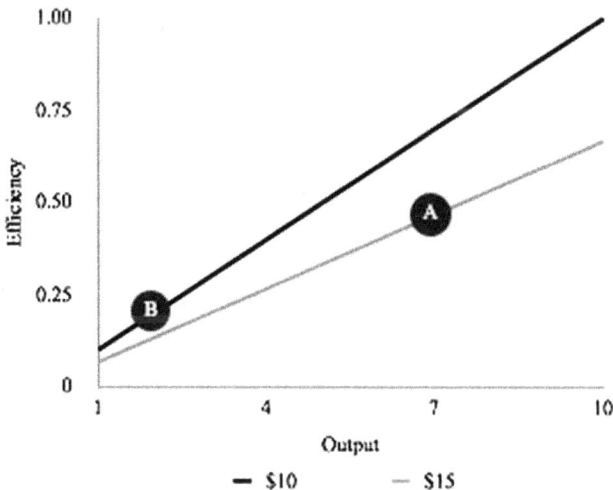

Exhibit A.3 *This picture tells the real story. When you do more with the same, you are more efficient. This chart shows you more efficient at $15 and handling seven than you are at $10 and handling two*

down. If at $10, your rep processes 10 calls versus eight, they were just more efficient. Cost$_{NC}$ goes down, which can lead those who are unaware down the wrong decision-making path.

I have seen a number of companies get into a significant amount of financial trouble not understanding this relationship. In the name of economies of scale, I've seen far too many people create too much output so they can "save money." When the output exceeds demand, you create waste. Companies have taken themselves to the brink of bankruptcy, if not beyond, believing if they can build more, do more, buy more, it will ultimately be cheaper. They are looking at cost$_{NC}$, not cost$_C$. According to the math, these actions may have negative implications for cost$_C$.

APPENDIX B

When considering the difference between being efficient and being productive, I tend to go back to the rectangles. The ideal situation is to have an overall balance between what is produced and what is needed, which I'll call demand. This is even true in constraint-based production such as when using constraint-based scheduling. The demand for each step should be designed around the needs of the constraints; hence, this demand may not be based and timed solely on the needs of a non-constraint resource. For instance, if I sign checks at 60 per hour and you can print them at 60 per minute, your demand may not be hourly based. Your demand may be determined to be 120 in two minutes so that you keep me busy for two hours and then move on to other needs.

When it comes to efficiency, I tend to look at it two ways. First, is the overall efficiency, comparing the output to input as discussed in Chapter 14. However, there is also a demand efficiency, comparing the demand to input. This allows you to do simple calculations and comparisons. First, you have actual efficiency, which is output/input (Equation B.1). Second, you can calculate the demand efficiency, or productivity, which I consider the ratio of demand to input. This is a modification of the efficiency equation (Equation B.2):

$$\text{Efficiency}_{\text{actual}}(e_a) = \text{Actual output / Input} \qquad (B.1)$$

$$\text{Efficiency}_{\text{demand}}(e_d) = \text{Demand / Input} \qquad (B.2)$$

From these two ratios, you can begin to tell a lot from your production and capacity situations. First, you can look at the absolute difference between your overall efficiency and your demand efficiency by taking the difference between the two (Equation B.3). This number can tell you how much capacity you either used too much of, or not enough of (Exhibit B.1). For instance, let's say you have eight hours, and in that eight hours, your employee, who manually puts return address labels on envelopes, should

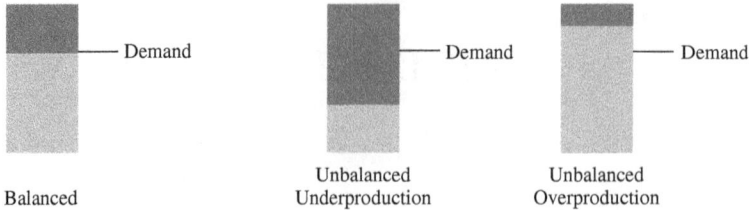

Exhibit B.1 *Ideally, you will want to balance your output with demand. Being unbalanced creates less than ideal situations. If you find you always have more capacity than there is demand for, this creates an opportunity to reduce cost$_C$ by reducing the amount of capacity you buy*

be able to process a maximum of 450 envelopes for an efficiency of 56.3 envelopes per hour. In one shift, she produces 400 envelopes. Her actual efficiency is 50 envelopes per hour. If demand is for 300 envelopes, the productivity level required for her is 37.5 envelopes per hour. From Equation B.3, she is 12.5 absolute efficiency points too high:

$$\text{Absolute efficiency difference} = e_a - e_d \qquad (B.3)$$

If the absolute difference is positive, that means you were too efficient. Being too efficient is not always a good thing. Doing excess work can create waste and, in some cases, increase your cost$_C$. If it is negative, it means you were not efficient enough. For example, if she only processed 240 envelopes, she would be 7.5 points too low (30 envelopes/hour -37.5 envelopes/hour $= -7.5$ envelopes/hour, a deficit).

You can also translate this into percent too high and too low as well using Equation B.4:

$$\% \text{ different} = (\text{absolute efficiency})/e_d * 100\% \qquad (B.4)$$

This equation will tell you how different efficiency and productivity are on a percentage basis.

What is important about these analyses is that the numbers give you a feel of how much over or under the demand levels you are, and this gives you options to adjust capacity levels of the efficiency of the capacity to meet demand.

Index

OTHER TITLES IN THE MANAGERIAL ACCOUNTING COLLECTION

Kenneth A. Merchant, University of Southern California, *Editor*

- *Value Creation in Management Accounting: Using Information to Capture Customer Value* by CJ McNair-Connolly, Lidija Polutnik, Riccardo Silvi, and Ted Watts
- *Breakeven Analysis: The Definitive Guide to Cost-Volume-Profit Analysis, Second Edition* by Michael E. Cafferky and Jon Wentworth
- *Revenue Management: A Path to Increased Profits, Second Edition* by Ronald J. Huefner
- *Cents of Mission: Using Cost Management and Control to Accomplish Your Goal* by Dale R. Geiger
- *Sustainability Reporting: Getting Started, Second Edition* by Gwendolen B. White

Announcing the Business Expert Press Digital Library

Concise e-books business students need for classroom and research

This book can also be purchased in an e-book collection by your library as

- a one-time purchase,
- that is owned forever,
- allows for simultaneous readers,
- has no restrictions on printing, and
- can be downloaded as PDFs from within the library community.

Our digital library collections are a great solution to beat the rising cost of textbooks. E-books can be loaded into their course management systems or onto students' e-book readers. The **Business Expert Press** digital libraries are very affordable, with no obligation to buy in future years. For more information, please visit **www.businessexpertpress.com/librarians.** To set up a trial in the United States, please email **sales@businessexpertpress.com.**

www.ingramcontent.com/pod-product-compliance
Lightning Source LLC
Chambersburg PA
CBHW060241230326
41458CB00094B/1400